THE HOLLYWOOD FEATURE FILM
IN POSTWAR BRITAIN

THE HOLLYWOOD FEATURE FILM IN POSTWAR BRITAIN

PAUL SWANN

ST. MARTIN'S PRESS
New York

© 1987 Paul Swann

All rights reserved. For information, write:
Scholarly & Reference Division,
St. Martin's Press, Inc., 175 Fifth Avenue, New York, NY 10010

First published in the United States of America in 1987

Printed in Great Britain

ISBN 0-312-00471-0

Library of Congress Cataloging-in-Publication Data

Swann, Paul.
    The Hollywood feature film in postwar Britain.

    Bibliography: p.
    Includes index.
    1. Moving-pictures — Great Britain — History.
2. Moving-pictures, American — Great Britain —
History. 3. Great Britain — Civilization — American
influences. 4. Great Britain — Popular culture.
I. Title.
PN1993.5.G7S89   1987   791.43'0941   86-26283
ISBN 0-312-00471-0

CONTENTS

1. Introduction   1

2. Americanization and Mass Culture   13

3. Three Pennyworth of Dark   31

4. Selling the American Way   51

5. American Stars and British Audiences   67

6. The Hollywood Embargo   81

7. US Cultural Policy in Postwar Britain   105

8. Britain's Postwar Film Policy   127

9. Conclusion: Britain and the Consumer Society   145

Select Bibliography   155

Index   164

Chapter One

Introduction

The ideological impact of Hollywood feature films shown in Britain in the decade after the Second World War offers an exploration of a very specific experience of cross-cultural exchange. The United States established cultural hegemony in Europe in conjunction with extending commercial and political/military control there. [1]

Europe has associated the United States with a commercial nexus since its birth, and often discussion of the American 'cultural invasion' has centred on the most commercialized of all cultural forms, the motion picture. 'Hollywood' is not only a geographical location. It is also an industry with its own standardized product, marketing and management practices, and specific conventions governing film structure and content. It is also constituted by the body of films made by the system during the last seventy years which have represented a relatively coherent social reality. Hollywood established its inter -national pre-eminence early on in the years between the two world wars. In most of the world, including virtually all of Europe, indigenous film production and film cultures were submerged beneath the weight of American financial control and its control of the high ground as far as narrative style was concerned. Technological developments in the areas of sound, colour, screen configuration and the like consolidated the American position.

Given the choice, audiences overseas have invariably preferred American films over those produced in their own country. Their position has generally been that American films are of 'higher quality' than those produced in their own country, but it has often been hard to pinpoint what particular qualities they mean.

In the years following the Second World War, the American government pursued a sophisticated cultural policy which extended furthest, in some respects, into the domain of motion pictures.

American propaganda often masqueraded as 'freedom of information' and the notion that showing the American way was truth or news - not propaganda. Hollywood collaborated in fighting the Cold War overseas as well as at home. Walter Wanger, an independent American producer, termed Hollywood's influence overseas 'a Marshall Plan of Ideas'. [2] American films occupied European cinema screens as effectively as American troops occupied the former battlefields.

This did not sit comfortably with the European intelligentsia. In the 1940s and 1950s many Europeans attacked 'Americanization' and 'standardization', which they felt were closely related phenomena These European critics adopted a vocabulary initially drawn from descriptions of the American approach to manufacturing and technology to explain what they saw as a similar American approach to social institutions and cultural forms. An array of American justifications and apologias for American policies and the actions of Americans in Europe dates from the same period. Both genres of writing have a long history. Chapter Two traces this tradition back to the nineteenth century, although its history goes back much further. But it was then that European and American commentators both began to acknowledge the major differences in the philosophies and societies emerging on opposite sides of the Atlantic. In broad terms, this was the nature of the debate: Europeans accused America of being a crassly commercial and intellectually and spiritually bankrupt society, whilst Europe was characterized as class-ridden, dilettante and living in the past. Comparisons between the relative standings of Athens and Rome and Europe and the United States were frequent. This is how Guido Piovene characterized the two positions:

(Europeans) looking upon America as simply a Europe across the sea . . . label everything that escapes their understanding as 'childish and barbaric'. Americans, on their side, consider themselves the offspring of Europe and fancy that when they have passed a summer holiday in their father's house, it can hold no secrets for them. [3]

Andre Visson, who had recently emigrated from France to the United States, placed blame for the growing rifts between the U.S. and Europe squarely with the Europeans. For him, these prejudices were based upon:

the fundamental, historic ignorance of America; the difficulty
of understanding the real differences between the European and
American conceptions of life; the too great emphasis on what
was queer, unusual, 'exotic' on the surface of American life,
the fundamental prejudice of the European intellectual elite
toward the American conception of the 'Common Man'; the
failure of Hollywood and the G.I.s to convey to the
Europeans a picture of the real America; the frustration that
comes from Europe's growing dependence on America's
wealth and power; the envy of America's newly acquired
wealth and power; the fear that America, intoxicated with her
wealth and power, and with her political and diplomatic
inexperience, may precipitate the world into the nightmare of
another war. [4]

In the 1950s and 1960s as America's commercial hegemony grew,
attacks levelled against Americanization gained impetus. Critical
assessments in these years tended to dwell upon commercial and
financial aspects of the American invasion, and specifically the
important consequences of the new communication technologies for
the extension of American control. Francis Williams argued that this
was fundamentally different from the forms of nineteenth century
European-style colonialism:

This American invasion differs, however, from the export of
ideas and modes of life which has always characterized
international societies in the broad front of its attack and the
forces of mass communication upon which it is able to call . .
. Their main purpose is to shape people into the pattern most
conforming to the requirements of salesmanship . . . The
British young get their conceptions of love, courtship,
marriage and family life, of dress, social etiquette and
professional success from Hollywood equally with the
American. [5]

The postwar discussion of Americanization often centred on the
American motion picture. The years after the war were the last decade
when film was the dominant mass medium and entertainment form in
Britain and the United States. The cinema occupied a position in
people's lives as a major social institution, analogous in some respects

3

to the central role of television today. Values and ideals were shared and celebrated in a ritual form, as people went each week to the movies. [6] However, watching television and seeing films are by no means identical experiences. Cinema was consciously purchased and consumed collectively, outside of the home and in the most artificial of circumstances. It could be argued that the film viewer was especially vulnerable in the temporary dream environment rented for a few hours. There was a compulsiveness to film watching, at least partly explained by the fact that cinema was one of the few luxury items never subject to rationing either during or after the war, but it went beyond this. Guy Morgan, for example, noted how during the blitz, people would brave all the hazards of the bombing to get to the cinema. [7]

Cinema was essentially a medium for predominantly working class audiences. All the evidence indicates that the cinema was still primarily aimed at this group throughout this period. As Mark Abrams noted: 'the working class and the young and the unmarried provide far and away the greater part of the money going into the Box Office'. [8] Movies were consumed communally in purpose-built structures and the 'content' of films spilled readily over into people's lives outside the cinema. Much that people had in common - the things that bound them together, the things that made them a society - were things learnt or acquired at the movies, as much as they were a part of Britain's organically based popular culture. Chapter Three explores why the British in the postwar decade were particularly susceptible to the influx of American culture and the manner in which they chose to appropriate and adopt it. This process of appropriation was not common to all classes in Britain.

Chapter Four suggests the substance of what it was that American films 'sold' in Great Britain. In both Britain and the United States, there was an acute awareness of the extent to which motion pictures served as advertisements for ideas as well as much more concrete items of merchandise. The governments of both countries were concerned about each kind of advertisement in equal measure. American films embodied a relatively coherent model of the ideal American community, which was as mythological to most Americans as it was to most British people. This myth underwent substantial changes in light of the events of the Cold War and a fairly pervasive pessimism about the prospects for American society. American films also encapsulated a vision of British society, and this also went through

4

significant changes during the postwar decade. Specifically, there was a retreat from any attempt to present contemporary British life in a realistic manner. American films about Britain were fixated upon either Britain's aristocracy, its empire or its past.

In the 1950s, there was a whole body of work devoted to studying the impact upon popular culture in Great Britain of the cultural production being imported from the United States. Richard Hoggart, Raymond Williams and others examined the changes taking place within British popular culture as a consequence of 'Americanization'. They saw traditional and folkloric cultural traditions increasingly supplanted by commercialized, reproducible and manufactured forms on American lines. Francis Williams argued: 'The British viewer is taking part in a surrender of the will to the concept of society as a captive mass audience, first attracted and then corrupted by the deliberate employment of superficial and meretricious modes of entertainment in order to induce a state of acquiescence to the most dishonest and fantastic commercial claims.' [9]

This was the context for my own childhood. I grew up in Rochdale, a town in the north of England, which had over a dozen cinemas in the fifties and only one some twenty years later. Like all my contemporaries, I never met an American, but saw many American films. Going to the cinema was a totalizing experience: the opulence of the buildings, the sheer size of the projected image itself, all buttressed, of course, by the fantasy nature of the films themselves, made the experience of cinema-going quite different from television and had an enormous impact upon British audiences. American films populated the British imagination to much greater effect than American television programmes a decade later.

American films did not 'mean' the same thing to British audiences as they did to the audiences in the United States. The two audiences drew upon very different cultural references when they decoded these films. Consequently, the images of America and Great Britain presented in American films could often be interpreted on different levels - one for the American audience, one for the British. Often films gained something, as well as losing something, in the transition/translation from America to Britain. The present study attempts to examine what these films did mean for the British people who watched them. The mythos of American films was vastly different from that of indigenously produced films, yet American films were almost invariably preferred by the British cinema audience.

Cinema was a principal form of pleasure for most people in the postwar decade. It is difficult to think of another pastime - the radio and smoking are the only ones which come readily to mind - which permeated so widely through different classes, regions, sexes and age groups. Listening to the radio involved few conscious expressions of choice, since it was not 'bought' in the sense that cinema tickets are bought and consequently was not a luxury in the way that smoking and the cinema were. Tobacco and films both came from the United States, and could only be purchased with precious dollars, and both were subject to immense government restraints and control, although only tobacco was subject to rationing.

The British were very faithful consumers of American films. In the mid-fifties, television had not begun to erode the cinema audience to a marked extent. In 1955, for example, annual average admissions in Great Britain were 22.7 million, down from 26.3 million in 1951. The much more drastic decline in admissions brought about by television came in the following two years; annual admissions in 1957 were 17.6 million, an annual percentage decline of 17%. [10] In the decade after the Second World War, the British were actually more loyal than the American cinema-goer to American films.

It is difficult to isolate the 'impact' of one specific cultural form from the general matrix of transatlantic cross-cultural transmission which has been such an important aspect of European-American relations since the Second World War. A number of recent studies of cultural imperialism have focused upon the consequences of American popular culture's globalization. [11] Ed Buscombe, for example, has spoken of the necessity of writing individual national cinema histories, and the extent to which this is only possible if national cinemas are viewed in reaction against Hollywood. [12]

Films and many other cultural forms were part of the changing *Zeitgeist* of Britain in the postwar decade. Britain in 1945 was a materially impoverished country. Its people faced nearly another decade of low living standards and cognitive deprivation before long-term recovery from the war began. Towards the end of this decade, Britain opted for an American-style consumer society. This was a surprising transformation. Like most revolutions, it was very quiet, although it did not pass unnoticed. As a Britain which had 'never had it so good' moved from austerity to affluence, commentators frequently noted that this affluence manifested itself via the motorcar, hire purchase and suburban housing developments, in an almost American way.

There were some associations between the British cinema audience and the Hollywood film which existed largely outside of both commercial considerations and the specific myths retailed in the storylines of the majority of American feature films. Chapter Five, for example, examines the nature of the relationship between American stars and British audiences, and the significance of these literally 'larger than life' fantasy figures for the British cinema-goer. Film stars combined the attributes of the typical and also the ideal personality type, and the notion of the star and the trappings of stardom were both a crucial part of Hollywood. Significantly, American stars were different in some very important ways from British stars. After the war, the British film industry, especially the Rank Organization, began to manufacture stars along American lines, but there remained very essential differences in the way in which British screen talent was presented to the British cinema audience both on and off the screen.

The film audience is that part of the cinematic apparatus which received fairly scant serious critical attention. A critical tradition which has emphasized the aesthetic and the political over the social has paid little regard to the preservation of sources for study of the cinema audience. Recent approaches to cultural studies centred on the spectator and consumer, such as reader-response criticism, and reception theory must now contend with the failure to preserve many of the valuable sources needed for this type of study.

An important source for this work is oral testimony. Many people who joined the hordes who went to the cinema in such great numbers can recall vividly their experiences, which gives some indication of the impression left by cinema-going at that time. Significantly, in oral histories attempting to document the experiences of the film audience, people are apt to talk as frequently about the experience of *going* to the cinema, and the setting within which they watched films as they do about the specifics of individual films and film stars. [13] The business of selling films and the desires of the film audience itself generated vast quantities of materials produced for the film audience in addition to the films themselves. There were many popular magazines devoted wholly or in part to the cinema. There were also many more specialized 'fan' magazines with a more obviously limited appeal.

There are very few extant runs of British fan magazines or popular film periodicals. The British Film Institute has some magazines of this nature, but its holdings are much poorer than its very extensive collections of film trade periodicals and art film journals. [14] This is despite the fact that the popular magazines had a much larger circulation than these other journals. *Kinematograph Weekly*, for example, had a circulation of under 7,000, whilst it has been estimated that in the early 1950s *Picturegoer* had a circulation of as much as 500,000. [15] Fortunately, the British Museum has a surprisingly extensive collection of popular film magazines, although even there the holdings are very sporadic.

The patchy nature of those materials produced for/by the film audience, compared to the masses of material generated for and by the film industry, the critic and the scholar, speaks volumes for critical approaches which have laboured over the creative process. However, until recently, little has been said about the nature of the experience(s) of the spectator. Popular film magazines from the postwar decade provide some insight into the group psyche of the postwar generation of film watchers. This is an important supplement to the work of social scientists and market researchers, whose findings are important sources for a later portion of this book.

This is not to argue that the spectator has been ignored, but that the focus on the act of consumption has tended to centre on the individual, rather than looking at the viewers *en masse*. Pyschoanalytical theory has been concerned with the essentially voyeuristic/scopophilic experience of film watching, and the role of desire in the viewing experience. [16] This, like similar approaches, has said relatively little about the collective nature of film watching. Hence, the current work is an attempt to explore the social nature of film watching within a very specific historical context and with a very narrow brief.

There have been many attempts to explore the impact of Hollywood's stylistic attributes upon British film production. There have also been studies of the intertwining of British and American films and film-makers. As has been chronicled most recently by Sheridan Morley, since the 1920s there has been a steady 'brain drain' of British talent - especially acting talent - to Hollywood. [17] There was also a long tradition of American production in Europe. In the thirties, this was basically a question of producing extremely cheap 'quota quickies' - to fulfil the terms of various Cinematograph Films Acts in Britain. Most European countries in the 1920s and 1930s were equally protectionist in their policies towards Hollywood. In postwar Britain, Anglo-American productions were increasingly common, especially after the British government prohibited American film producers from taking the bulk of their earnings out of the country, which obliged the American studios to produce an increasing number of films in Great Britain. A number of other European countries placed similar restraints on American producers, resulting in a number of co-production ventures, as well as a series of enterprising schemes to convert ostensibly non-convertible currencies into dollars to get film rental revenues back to the United States. This resulted in some interesting films, but in general the resulting co-productions, which drew their principal talent from the United States and the rest of the cast and locations from Britain, were uninspired films, very much in the tradition of the old 'quota quickies'. There was also a recurrent fear - largely actualized in recent years - that Britain would become a mere production facility for Hollywood, with the profits going to the United States.

It is hard to exaggerate the importance of Britain as a market for Hollywood. For nearly 40 years, Britain was Hollywood's biggest export market. In 1946, for example, between them, the United States and Great Britain accounted for 120 million out of the 235 million worldwide cinema admissions each week, 30 million of these being in Britain. [18] The impact of television upon the motion picture industry in the United States, which was felt several years earlier than in Great Britain, made Hollywood producers constantly more dependent on their share of the British market. As *Fortune* magazine noted in 1948: 'In the peculiar economics of the industry, British revenues frequently spell the difference between profits and loss for American film companies.' [19]

There was a very long tradition of protectionism and interventionism on the part of the British government. After the Second World War, possessed by the absolute necessity of stemming the tide of dollars spent on imported luxuries , amongst other desperate measures, the Labour government tried to institute very extensive financial control over the product of the American film industry in Britain, when for the first time it taxed the gross revenues of the American film distributors.   The American response to this challenge

9

to a major part of its export trade was a boycott of the British film market - the only time when there was a conscious decision on the part of the film industry to withhold films from the British market. Ultimately, this was a major victory for the American industry. Chapter Six examines in detail the battle between the American film industry and the British government.

After 1945, the United States government was compelled to proselytize actively overseas, using every informational tool at its disposal. Chapter Seven explores some of the means used by the American government to further its own ends in Great Britain by dictating the policies of the British government and influencing British public opinion. American motion pictures were widely acknowledged as a significant part of the government's postwar international information policy, and there was a fair degree of collusion between the American government and the American film industry in their actions overseas.

Chapter Eight examines the 'film policy' pursued by the British government in the postwar decade. This was tied to the country's need for economic and social reconstruction, but was tempered by the ongoing concern about the nature of the 'impact' of the American film, indeed of all aspects of American popular culture, upon postwar British society. This concern tended to focus upon the sort of effect which Hollywood films were thought to have upon the young and the less well-educated. Films had been the centre of this debate in Britain since the 1920s. Interestingly, in the years after the war researchers from the United States, both scholars and market researchers, began attempting to gauge empirically the effects of American mass culture in other countries . George Gallup moved his operation to Britain and Herbert Gans was one of the first to focus specifically on the impact of the American mass media overseas. [20] Their work is an important source for this text. They tried to assess and evidence the impact of their country's cultural exports, generally from a straightforward behavioural position.

Chapter Nine attempts to suggest what part was played by the American feature film as a harbinger of American-style popular culture in the evolution of British social and cultural life in the postwar decade. This is perhaps best understood as part of a general action taking place on a very broad front, for the feature film was the most conspicuous manifestation of the globalization of American popular culture after the war. There were clearly attempts by the American government and the film industry itself to use the feature film as 'propaganda', but in much more subtle and pervasive ways American feature films sold an ideology and a world view which were very seductive to postwar Europe and nowhere more so than in Britain.

Notes

1. A. Gramsci, *Prison Notebooks: Selections*, trans. Q. Hoare, G. N. Smith, (International Publishers, New York, 1971).
2. W. Wanger, 'Donald Duck and Diplomacy', *Public Opinion Quarterly*, vol. 14, no. 2 (1950), p. 444.
3. G. Piovene, 'Ungrateful Europe', in J. Burnham (ed.), *What Europe Thinks of America* (John Day, New York, 1953), p. 111.
4. A. Visson, *As Others See Us* (Doubleday, Garden City, New Jersey, 1948), pp. 232 - 3.
5. F. Williams, *The American Invasion* (Crown, New York, 1962), p. 35. E. A. McCreary, *The Americanisation of Europe* (Doubleday, New York, 1964) is another good example of this literature.
6. E. Durkheim, *Elementary forms of the Religious Life*, trans. J. W. Swain (Free Press, Glencoe, 1965).
7. G. Morgan, *Red Roses Every Night* (Quality Press, London, 1948).
8. M. Abrams, 'The British Cinema Audience, 1949', *Hollywood Quarterly*, vol. 4, no. 3 (1950) p. 252.
9. Williams, *American Invasion*, p. 36.
10. Political and Economic Planning, *The British Film Industry*, (PEP, London, 1958) , p. 135.
11. C. W. E. Bigsby, Superculture: American Popular Cultture and Europe (Elek, London, 1975); D. Hebdige, Towards a Cartography of Taste 1935 - 1962', in B. Waites, T. Bennett and G. Martin (eds.), *Popular Culture: Past and Present* (Croom Helm, Beckenham, 1983).
12. E. Buscombe, 'Film History and the Idea of a National Cinema', *Australian Journal of Screen Theory*, nos. 9/10 (1981), pp. 141-153.
13. I am indebted to Joanne Burke and the other students in my film

history class at Temple University in the Spring 1985 semester for their work gathering oral testimony concerning the experiences of film audiences in Philadelphia in the 1920s and 1930s.

14. A. Slide (ed.), *International Film, Radio and Television Journals* (Greenwood Press, London, 1985) is an invaluable guide to film trade, art and audience-oriented periodicals.

15. B. Baker, 'Picturegoes', *Sight and Sound,* vol. 53, no. 3 (1985), pp. 206 - 1, is a rare look at fan literature.

16. L. Mulvey, 'Visual Pleasure and Narrative Cinema', *Screen* (1975), reprinted in B. Nichols (ed.), *Movies and Methods* (University of California Press, Los Angeles, 1985) vol. 2.

17. S. Morley, *Tales from the Hollywood Raj: The British, the Movies and Tinseltown* (Viking Press, New York, 1984).

18. R. Manvell, 'Recent Films', *Britain Today*, April 1946.

19. *Fortune*, June 1948.

20. H. Gans, 'American Films and Television Programs on British screens: A Study of the Functions of American Popular Culture Abroad' unpublished PhD dissertation, University of Pennsylvania, 1959.

Chapter Two

Americanization and Mass Culture

'Americanization' is a concept with a long history, arguably, as Jim Potter has noted, most commonly used in an economic and industrial sense. [1] The connotations of Americanization have included commercial nexus and the profit motive, efficiency and standardization, but also equality of opportunity, energy and youth - or immaturity, depending on the observer's outlook. There is also a history of comparisons between the 'New World' and the 'Old World', which, depending on the position of the observer, have criticized either the American or the European model. Inevitably, such comparisons have suffered from breadth and generalization. Usually they have taken the form of attempts to see what each continent could learn from the mistakes and successes of the other. [2]

A body of work with an equally long history consists of assessments of the impact of Americanization in Europe. This chapter focuses upon British assessments of Americanization. Britain was initially responsible for populating North America, and for shaping its political, its social and its cultural institutions. Britain was also, as the first industrial nation, the initial model for modern industrial society, and this, along with parliamentary-style democracy, made profound impressions upon the development of America in the nineteenth century. Consequently, although the majority of Americans cannot trace their origins back to Great Britain, Britain has always been the mother country to a greater extent than any other single European power. This, together with the manner in which the United States has gradually assumed the imperial mantle of Great Britain, has perhaps made the British more preoccupied with the phenomenon of Americanization than any other European nation. Matthew Arnold's belief that 'The rise of the democracy to power in America and Europe is not, as has been hoped, to be a safeguard of peace and civilisation. It is the rise of the uncivilised, whom no school education can suffice to

13

provide with intelligence and reason' had a long history. [3]

European anxieties about 'Americanization' began in the middle of the last century. From an early date, these anxieties focused upon the mass and urban nature of America's culture and society. As Patrick Brantlinger has recently noted, theories of mass culture have tended to associate the emergence of such cultures with moral and/or social decay. [4] Starting at the beginning of this century, Americanization became increasingly synonymous with advanced forms of industrial production and the mass culture which this type of social organization permitted. Polemics against Americanization centred upon what were the new technologies of that era, and their dire social and cultural consequences. In this century, the impact of the United States overseas as a model for others and as a power in its own right focused attention on the economic, political and social aspects of Americanization. In Britain, in fact, commercial considerations historically have always been paramount in discussing the impact of American popular culture there.

In Britain, discussion of the influence of American-style mass culture has always been very common. In a recent issue of *Punch* , for example, there is a piece on the detrimental effect on the British theatre of the presence of large numbers of American tourists in British theatres, which is felt to have brought down the level of dramatic productions. The biggest successes in the West End in 1985 were Hollywood-style musicals, like *Oklahoma*, featuring American talent.[5] This is absolutely typical of the position taken by British critics, who have invariably concentrated upon the adverse effects of American culture upon British culture. In the 1930s and 1940s, commentary often focused upon two related areas: the American feature film, generally regarded as the most conspicuous example of cross-cultural transmission; and discussion of the American influence upon written and spoken English.

The feature film was generally regarded as the most conspicuous and pernicious example of American mass culture in Britain. Consequently, polemics against the harmful consequences of American culture often used the feature film as a bell-wether for Americanization in general. As the British historian, D. W. Brogan noted:

Members of Parliament talked with indignation and alarm of the

the dire influence of American films; not since 1066 or 1588
had English civilisation been in greater danger and, with only a
little touching up, one might have taken some parliamentary
voices for those of Goebbels, Gayda and Goga . [6]

European intellectuals of all political persuasions felt that the
United States' mass and materially based culture constituted a concerted
attack upon both the 'high' culture of the intellectual/social elite and
the native 'folk' cultures of their population as a whole. In Britain,
comments about the 'new materialism' and 'levelling down' associated
with Americanization started in the 1890s and reached a crescendo in
the 1930s in the work of T. S. Eliot, Frank and Q. D. Leavis and
other members of the traditional literary establishment. As Andre
Visson put it, with perhaps only slight exaggeration: 'the majority of
British intellectuals . . . have always been ready to lend an ear to any
witness bringing from the United States new evidence of American
vulgarity and inferiority'. [7] A conference on transatlantic cultural
relations held under the auspices of UNESCO in Geneva in 1954
commented on this process:

> Americanization involves a general raising of the standard of
> living, for which the man in the street certainly has no cause
> to complain. But it is inevitably accompanied by a certain
> social 'levelling' which cannot be expected to be entirely
> satisfactory to the elite. [8]

Essayists frequently returned to the question of the impact of
American-style mass society, and specifically commoditized and
manufactured popular culture. In other words, culture that was created
for, not by, the people who consumed it. Prior to the war, F. R.
Leavis and his cadre of literary critics attacked the American influence
on the grounds that it was essentially and innately foreign (always a
good criticism in Britain!) and alien to British traditions, which were
properly organically bedded in the societies which created them. In
Culture and Anarchy, Culture and Environment, and Q. D. Leavis'
Fiction and the Reading Public, they compared the community-based
traditions of nineteenth century agrarian Britain with the shallow style
and content of contemporary commercial literature. [9] *Culture and
Environment* was intended initially as a text for high school English
courses, and was specifically interested in the manner in which

15

advertising copywriting styles and mass market fiction had diluted the standards of English literature.

Since the mid-nineteenth century, a battle had been pending between the proponents of European high culture, Matthew Arnold, Oswald Spengler, Arnold Toynbee and latterly Leavis, T. S. Eliot and Jose Y. Gasset de Ortega, and the forces of mass culture, led by F. W. Woolworth and Louis B. Mayer. The New World/Old World dichotomy lent itself to easy polarities. European intellectuals thought the United States was a bastard civilization: 'American culture is a veneer, whereas European culture is ingrained.' [10] In late nineteenth century Britain, Matthew Arnold had championed the culture of the best and had attacked the 'crudities of the industrialism of his age'. [11] The Arnoldian tradition, one of the rare schools of literary criticism which judged work in its social and historical context, saw America as synonymous with all that was wrong with industrialization, commerce and democracy. [12] Democracy implied equality, and, if all things were equal, then this invalidated the elitist intentions of the Arnoldian school. Industrialization produced a secularized society and state of mind in which there was little time or need for philosophical reflection, which was felt to create as D. H. Lawrence noted of his native East Midlands: 'a gap in the continuity of consciousness, almost American, but industrial really'. [13]

Patrick Brantlinger has recently discussed the tradition of 'negative classicism' in the following terms: 'Conservative theorists also tend to see mass culture as mechanical rather than organic, secular rather than sacred, commercial rather than free or unconditioned, plebeian or bourgeois and vulgar rather than aristocratic and "noble"; based on self-interest rather than on high ideals, or appealing to the worst instincts in people rather than the best, cheap and shoddy rather than enduring, imitative rather than original and urban, bureaucratic and centralised rather than close to nature, communal and individualised.'[14]

The United States was regarded by Europe's cultural elite not as the land of opportunity, but as a country barren of both history and traditions, and populated by her own cast-offs. This is a tradition which can be traced back to the eighteenth century, when Buffon had maintained that America was an inferior continent, populated by inferior animal and human stock, and destined to deteriorate. Later commentaries saw American culture as urban, not urbane, centred on a cash nexus rather than any deep spiritual basis. European thinkers regarded this as a major threat to their own culture. Oswald Spengler, for example, saw in the United States 'a tendency to flaccid thinking and mediocre intelligence, dominated by media which in turn are manipulated by the money forces.' [15] Culture, like everything else it was thought, had fallen into the province of big business and industry in the United States. Sinclair Lewis's *Babbitt* was widely thought to be an accurate portrayal of the state of the arts in the United States: 'In other countries, art and literature are left to a lot of shabby bums living in attics and feeding on booze and spaghetti, but in America the successful artist or picture painter is indistinguishable from any other decent businessman.' [16]

When American popular culture's artifacts and entertainments geared to mass tastes rather than traditionally defined aesthetic and social standards began to percolate into Europe in large quantities, in the twentieth century, it seemed as if many classical pessimists' worst fears were confirmed. Europeans, reacting violently to the behaviour of American G.I.s in postwar Europe, saw the influence of black culture and the 'culture of the redman' in 'jazz blared out from dawn to midnight, was a certain type of motion picture, was anti-intellectualism, was an infantile, purely quantitative sex mania given to festooning a sequence of temporarily cherished squaws with bracelets and beads'. [17] American-style mass production and standardization, especially when they spilled over into the domain of culture, were thought ultimately to be very destructive: 'Mass production has turned out to involve standardisation and levelling down outside the domain of mere material goods.' [18]

The authorities assembled by UNESCO perceived a growing chasm between Europe and the USA in the immediate postwar years. They attributed this to America's economic strength, compared with their own exhaustion, and feared that America was not sufficiently mature for the role of global leader which it was rapidly acquiring. They were fairly pessimistic about the prospects for a mutually beneficial cultural exchange between the US and Europe. Instead, they prophesised an impending global acceptance of American culture and the complete subversion of the indigenous cultures.

In the context of the Cold War, the United States had to be made more attractive than the Soviet Union. Meanwhile:

> Europe and even Latin America often accuse the United States of inundating them with a low type of literature, a kind of pre-digested intellectual (or so-called intellectual) food, commercial films, and soulless mechanical devices. We are right to rebel and defend ourselves against such things, but we are often unjust in believing that they constitute the United States' sole contribution. [19]

J. B. Priestley coined the evocative term 'admass' to describe the way in which American-style mass culture emerged in Britain after the war. George Orwell was another who thought that the American influence was, on the whole, detrimental. For Orwell, traditional British folk culture was very different from the synthetic product consumed by the Americans:

> We are a nation of flower-lovers, but also a nation of stamp-collectors, amateur carpenters, coupon snippers, darts players, crossword puzzle fans. All the culture that is most truly native centres around things which even when they are communal are not official - the pub, the football match, the back garden, the fireside and the 'nice cup of tea'. [20]

The early development of the motion picture had initially followed the traditional currents of cultural trade. At the beginning of this century, there was a genuinely international market in popular culture. Buffalo Bill and his Indians entertained the industrial workers of Manchester and the crowned heads of Europe, whilst Chaplin and Stan Laurel were like many European music hall acts who toured the United States. European stars like Charles Dickens and Jenny Lind also performed regularly in the United States. Buffalo Bill and his colleagues, aided by a popular literature, created an idealized vision of America for Europeans. [21] The image of America and American society which Europeans created for themselves was an important part of their ideology. Europe's lower classes fixed the image of America as cornucopia in their minds, an image which was quite at odds with that of the intelligentsia. By 1918, large-scale migration from Europe to the United States was over, but the relatives of families in the

United States and its popular culture beckoned constantly.

During the First World War, the United States conquered the world's market for motion pictures. Recent migrants to the United States like Adolph Zukor and William Fox learnt how to produce films which appealed to the American and European audiences more than European films.

The motion picture evolved into a quintessentially American cultural form: based on advanced technology, not simple artists' tools, and yielding well to commercial exploitation. Hollywood developed along industrial lines, with standardization, specialization of labour and many other ways of obtaining economies of scale. As Walter Benjamin noted, it was a form which thrived on the capabilities of mechanical reproduction. In common with other industrialized forms of entertainment, such as the player piano and the gramophone, the motion picture separated artist and audience, or manufacturer and consumer. This was an important characteristic of reproducible forms: that they could reproduce precisely the same experience *ad infinitum,* anywhere, at any time, on demand. [22] Consequently, film, like these other forms, could be marketed in a manner impossible for early vehicles for popular culture. The ability to reproduce the same experience for film viewers all over the world meant that it was possible to create a truly international market for film, in a way that was impossible for any other form of cultural production.

America conquered Europe's film markets by catering to the tastes of audiences who had probably never heard of Matthew Arnold or Frank Leavis. In Britain in the 1920s, as in so many European countries, Hollywood films regularly accounted for more than 90% of British screentime. [23] They were self-evidently very popular with the lay public. Provincial cinema audiences in England were more familiar with the urban landscapes and rural wildernesses of the United States than they were with the south of England. As D. W. Brogan noted: 'The British consumer with a constancy that should delight Professors von Misses, Hayek and Robbins has, when given a chance, chosen to spend his sixpence or a shilling on poison from Hollywood instead of on the more wholesome and duller British product.' [24]

American feature films were invariably viewed as a 'threat' by the British elite. They sold American goods, services and ideas throughout the world, but nowhere were they more successful at this than within the British Empire. Will Hays, head of the Motion Picture Association

19

of America and Sir Philip Cunliffe-Lister, President of the British Board of Trade, were equally conscious of the 'indirect publicity' value which accrued from feature films, which Hays, probably in a gross understatement, estimated as 'one foot of film equalling one dollar of trade'. [25] It was also regarded as a *sine qua non* that an empire, to validate its imperial standing, ought to impose its own culture and values on its subjects, and prevent the infiltration of outside cultural influences. As a *Kine Weekly* editorial noted in 1930:

> It is horrible to think that the British Empire is receiving its education from a place called Hollywood. The Dominions would rather have a picture with a wholesome, honest British background, something that gives British sentiment, something that is honest to our traditions, than the abortion which we get from Hollywood. [26]

Though economic issues were paramount in these discussions, there was also a pervasive sense that film ought to be appropriated as a part of the national culture of the country.

Until the1930s, high art - 'Culture' with a capital 'C' - was, almost by definition, European. American artists and authors had to come to Europe if they wanted to be at the centre of modern art - very much as they must come to New York or London today. Paris, London and Berlin were the hub of the international literary and artistic world. Henry James was perhaps the paradigm of this, but he was joined by many fellow Americans: Man Ray, T. S. Eliot, the Fitzgeralds, Hemingway and many others. Henry James wrote about the complete necessity for the American artist to come to terms with Europe: 'He must deal more or less, even if only by implication, with Europe, whereas no European is obliged to deal in the least with America.' [27]

This was perhaps hyperbole; the 'old world versus the new' issue had been a central feature of cultural life in both Europe and North America since the middle of the last century. However, it was certainly true, that if one talked about the international market in the work and reputations of the cultural world, then Europe in essence dominated. America was still regarded as parochial and a backwater. In contrast, it was clearly a sign of the times in the postwar literary world when W. H. Auden returned from self-imposed exile in the United States in the uniform of an American major. [28] This was a clear indication of Europe's diminished position in global culture.

All the connotations of traditional definitions of high culture were innately and unashamedly elitist and exclusive. Consequently, it was some considerable time before film was regarded as in any sense an art form, tied as it was to mass entertainment. In the thirties, however, the notion of film as art emerged: Soviet realism, British documentary, the experiments of the surrealists and other branches of the avant-garde, were all instances of film being elevated to the status of an art form. However, in each of these cases, artistic respectability was bought at the expense of repudiating accessibility and the mass audience. The commercial cinema, on the other hand, did not really become respectable in intellectual circles until after it had ceased to be the predominant mass visual medium.

In the interwar years, films aimed at the popular audience were not regarded as art - they were generally dismissed as cheap sensationalist entertainment. Films were regarded, in the words of Leavis and Thompson, as 'substitute living', a seductive form of shallow but unsatisfying escape which they felt had come to dominate industrial culture:

> This form of compensation . . . is the very reverse of
> recreation, in that it tends not to strengthen and refresh the
> addict for living, but to increase his unfitness by habituating
> him to weak evasions, to the refusal to face reality at all. [29]

This kind of position was responsible in large part for the emergence of the documentary impulse in British film-making and literature in the 1930s and 1940s, which can be viewed as a concerted attempt to make the viewer 'face reality'. The cinema was the first major cultural form which originated outside the traditional sources of cultural production. It was damned in the eyes of Leavis *et al.* by its origins in nineteenth century entertainment, as well as its links with mechanical reproduction and commerce. All these placed the motion picture closer to, say, an advertisement for patent medicine or a Ford motor car than to fine painting or poetry. The commercial nature of the American feature film and its reliance upon mass appeal rendered it debased and debasing for the defenders of the traditional arts. On these grounds, the cinema was even debasing than hack mass market fiction, because it was completely passive and involved no real engagement on

21

the part of the viewer comparable to the experience of the reader. [30]

This type of adversarial position tended to predicate the intellectual establishment's response to the American feature film. Commentary tended to take the form of assessing the damage done to the country's moral and social fabric by these films, rather than a discussion of their aesthetic merits. In both North America and England, during the postwar decade, films from the continent were much more likely to be regarded as art than anything produced by Hollywood.

Perhaps the most frequent comments about American films dealt with their supposed homogenizing effect. It was commonly held that external differences in dress, speech and demeanour, which had previously been clear demarcators of class and background in Britain, were increasingly ambiguous. George Orwell, for example, believed American films had educated the British working class in these things. Films and television were thought to make the 'same accents, manners and fashions accepted from Land's End to Berwick'. [31] On the other hand, it was also generally thought that American speech patterns and idioms had had a detrimental effect:

> American has gained a footing in England partly because of
> the vivid, almost poetic quality of its slang, partly because
> certain American usages save time, and most of all, because
> one can adopt an American word without crossing a class
> barrier . . . To the working class . . . the use of
> Americanisms is a way of escaping from Cockney without
> adopting the BBC dialect, which they instinctively dislike
> and cannot easily master. Hence, especially in the big
> towns, working class children now use American slang from
> the moment that they learn to talk. [32]

Many agreed with Chancellor Hugh Dalton that Britain in the age of austerity, the Anglo-American loan and the mandatory return to full convertibility of sterling could afford 'bacon but not Bogart'. Remittances to America, particularly for the sale of luxury items like cigarettes and films, figured prominently in discussions of economic crises which plagued the country throughout the decade. At one point, the chancellor noted that the sum total of British exports to the United States was worth less than the value of American tobacco sales alone in this country.

Hollywood films were widely thought the prime example of Britain living beyond its means. Major political figures like Stafford Cripps, Hugh Dalton and Hugh Gaitskell stumbled over the intricacies of film finance and industrial regulation, whilst another, Harold Wilson, a very young President of the Board of Trade, rose to prominence by mastering them.

After the Second World War, the perennial debate about the economic and social impact of the American feature film in Britain was highlighted by the fact that many Britons and Americans had come into contact with each other *en masse* for the first time during the war. Bases like the huge American supply and maintenance base at Burtonwood in Lancashire became American cities inside Great Britain, complete with baseball diamonds, snack bars, beauty shops and 'washeterias'. The recent spate of new books about British GI brides is a belated recognition of one of the many ways in which America shaped Europe in very profound ways during the war.

The American presence in Europe was sustained after 1945 by the large standing armies left there and also in the growing hordes of American tourists who visited each year. Harry Hopkins, following Defoe, Orwell and Priestley, wrote a travel diary for a journey through Britain in the early 1950s. Regularly he encountered '*Americanus Turisticus*, in pearly-grey hat, hung about with leicas and light meters', and '*Americanus G.I. Joe*, fresh-faced and crew-cut, rimless and earnest, bursting, as usual, in sheer rude health, out of those sleek blue Air Force uniforms'. [33] The number of American tourists visiting Europe soon came to equal the total number of European migrants to North America. Never before had there been such a potential for cross-cultural contact between the people of different continents. The presence of American tourists reinforced the growing concern about the impact of American popular culture in Europe.

At the same time, Marshall Aid, the Anglo-American Loan, and the Berlin Airlift served to reiterate one of the principal themes of American popular culture in Europe: the United States as the land of plenty and opportunity. In Italy, for example: 'The popular ideal of America, particularly among the humbler classes, was that of a land where living and working conditions were much better than they were in Italy, and wealth was much easier to acheive. Even for the Italians who stayed in Italy the United States symbolised redemption from poverty and hope for a better future.' [34] In Britain, the situation was less straightforward, and Britain had a more complicated client status with the United States than Italy. As the United States' principal ally, Britain was obliged to fulfil many overseas and military obligations which it could ill-afford. Britain did not terminate rationing until July 1954 - over nine years after the end of the war. Expenditure on defence, and especially the war in Korea, was cited as a major factor depressing the British standard of living, and the United States was often held to blame for this. Sometimes the connections were very direct. For example, the raising of National Health charges to pay for defence commitments brought the resignation of the Minister of Health, Aneurin Bevan.

America's authority in Europe in the postwar decade was not like traditional forms of imperialism. Control was not vested in great armies, nor big navies - although the United States had both as well as, for a time, a monopoly on the atomic bomb. America's dominion was cultural and economic. In the 1940s, American business acumen and entrepreneurial skills launched the United States into an unparalleled and unprecedented economic lead. In the years that followed, Europeans widely believed that this was the only model for their own economic recovery. The Anglo-American Council on Productivity, which made its report in 1952, maintained that Britain must follow the methods of the United States in manufacturing and marketing. [35] The United States' capital investment and share of the markets in Europe continued to grow into the 1960s, producing a spate of books which attempted to explain the Americans' prowess and assessing the damage done to Europe's economies. Jacques Servan-Schreiber argued that America had essentially subverted Europe's economic strength by taking it over. He noted that, after the United States, perhaps the biggest single concentration of capital investment in industry resided in American investment within Europe, and that 90% was paid for out of Europe's own resources. [36] Servan-Schreiber argued that the United States' success stemmed from an educational system which encouraged technological training and research, business as a serious academic field and team spirit tempered by individual effort. John Ney, writing five years later, argued for the obverse, maintaining that Europe's failures - and especially Britain's - were essentially a consequence of the degeneration of the social fabric of countries which had embarked upon a form of senility. [37]

America's control in Europe was also cultural. Throughout the western world and Latin America, national leaders watched in dismay as American popular culture supplanted their own. America's films occupied Europe's screens, and pop music Europe's airwaves, as effectively as American troops occupied the former battlefields. It was commonly believed that America and its cultural artifacts were young and immature, and it certainly seems that younger and less affluent Europeans were most susceptible to American popular culture: teenagers in Manchester, Munich and Milwaukee all learnt to wear the same clothes, to do and say the same things. A genuinely international youth culture was being forged - but very much along American lines.

Teenagers were a relatively small section of society. As a subculture, they achieved a distinct group identity only in the years after the war. Conceptually, the notion of the teenager was something that was largely learned from the United States, and in the 1950s in Britain there emerged a whole genre of books on the problem of the teenager and the juvenile delinquent - itself another term also taken from the United States. Mark Abrams observed the way in which British teenagers drew upon role models in the United States: 'Postwar Britain has little experience in providing for prosperous working class teenagers; the latter have therefore, in shaping their `consumption standards and habits, depended very heavily on the one industrial country that has such experience, the United States.' [38]

In Britain, the growth of American-style modes of speech and behaviour, of an interest in 'the soulless mechnical devices' regarded as the hallmark of the American way, were widely noted in the postwar decade as part of the process of Americanization. A number of social surveys evidenced the changes in postwar Britain, utilizing polling techniques devised during the war and influenced by the emergence of ethnography and anthropology as serious academic disciplines. Studies by Richard Hoggart and Willmott and Young emphasized the way in which traditonal working class communities were breaking down and being re-shaped, either by the new cultural forces they were facing, or because of the social engineering and planning which was rearranging people's lives for them. [39]

Is it possible to gauge the impact of the transmission of American cultural values in feature films as part of these postwar changes in British society? This was a period when Britain's international standing and indigenous culture went through dramatic transformations. The

Britain of 1945 was hardly recognizable in the relatively sleek consumerist society which existed a decade later. In 1945, Britain was exhausted by a long war - as well as the depression which had preceded it. Yet it was obliged to maintain large standing armies in the Middle and Far East, the Balkans and elsewhere. Britain also faced acute material shortages, but had immediately embarked upon a massive reconstruction campaign. The Labour government began the long process of dismantling the Empire and a complete reappraisal of Britain's international standing. During the postwar decade, there were tremendous accomplishments under Attlee's administration, especially in the areas of social welfare and industrial reconstruction. Thereafter, beginning in 1952, after nearly a decade of hard times for most of the population, the country embarked upon a consumerist binge. Significantly for this study, perhaps the paradigm consumer item became the television set. The new era was hailed as a 'New Elizabethan Age', which was signalled by the complete abolition of rationing and more symbolically by the coronation of Elizabeth II. This period of 'new materialism' seemed very similar to that which had been endemic in the United States since the 1920s. Suddenly, people began demanding consumer durables which were qualitatively quite different from those of their forebears. These commodities were available and a culture had emerged which defined people's lives partly in terms of how they consumed.

Britain in 1945 was stolidly committed to a socialist experiment, mass nationalization, wholesale national reconstruction and a 'cradle to grave' welfare system. A decade later, individualism and consumerism, not socialism, were in vogue.

The present study attempts to relate postwar changes in Britain to cultural transmisson from the United States during that time. The motion picture was one of many elements in this exchange, and arguably was the most profound instance of the manner in which the United States colonized the imagination of Europe after the war. Tom Guback had discussed some aspects of America's conquest of the European film industry. [40] His important study focuses upon the economics of American control and pays relatively little attention to the content of American films in Europe, or the manner in which they impacted upon European audiences.

In the postwar decade, the United States worked to recreate former enemy nations in its own image. Britain ostensibly was America's principal ally during and after the war, but a very impoverished one which found it increasingly difficult to shoulder the burden of overseas defence commitments. During this period, Americanization also meant recruitment for American interests overseas. American policies entailed substantial aid for Britain, but at a cost which was usually higher than that levied upon the other former allies and belligerent powers. American aid to Britain ultimately entailed massive devaluation of sterling, the eventual demise of 'Imperial Preference' and the erosion of the sterling area.

American values and ideas were appropriated in a spectacular fashion in postwar Britain, especially by those people who were the most vulnerable to outside influences. On the whole, these tended to be drawn from the industrial workforce, who bore the brunt of shortages and long hours in the war and the post-1945 export war. A very powerful argument against limits on American film imports was that such restrictions would make industrial workers' morale suffer.

It is hard to measure the degree of alienation experienced by people after the war, but there are some guidelines. For example, George Gallup found that over half the people he surveyed in the 25-35 age group would emigrate if they had the opportunity. [41] A proposal that the entire population of the country should move to Canada was also seriously mooted. There were massive waiting lists for all those countries which permitted migration - though, significantly, the quotas allocated to the British for migration to the United States were rarely (and are rarely) filled. This separation from traditional social/cultural values drew the British - especially the working classes - to the values of other countries, and especially the coherent representation of a different society offered by American popular culture.

It has often been argued that Americanization was progressive, in the sense that it began with the working classes and percolated up through the social hierarchy. As Karl Meyer wrote in 1968, when talking about the Beatles - a British working class phenomenon with a great following in the United States at that time:

> The (British) lower classes were the first to be openly
> Americanized and they pass it on with their accents . . . The
> flat fact is that the Beatles and rest of the lower class gave up
> on English models and began imitating America utterly. [42]

Herbert Gans, in a study focusing upon British consumption of American films and television programmes in the 1950s, argued that many working class people had become alienated from traditional British values partially as a consequence of the example of American popular culture which they saw in American feature films. The state of Britain in the postwar years made them very susceptible to the aspiration fantasies and the classless/regionless society they saw at the cinema. Gans believed this explained why the British working class preferred American films to those produced in their own country. They provided 'themes that appeal to aspirations of the young British working class, whereas the British films and their creators are more concerned with the preoccupations of the middle-aged, middle class audience'. [43]

They presented a vision of a classless/regionless society, a model for upward social mobility in a consumer society which was very powerful and seductive. T.S. Eliot maintained that consumerism and consumption-centred life, based on rationally organized industrial production, which he termed Fordism, was the United States' major contribution to the notion of a new society. This certainly seemed a significant part of the model which was presented to postwar Britain.

Notes

1. J. Potter, ' "You Too Can Have Statistics Like Mine" : Some Economic Comparisons', in R. Rose (ed.), *Lessons from America: An Exploration* (John Wiley, New York, 1974), p. 94.
2. M. Cunliffe, 'New World, Old World: The Historical Antithesis', in Rose, *Lessons from America*.
3. Charles Norton to Leslie Stephen, 8 January 1896, cited in T. S. Eliot, 'Matthew Arnold', in D. J. DeLaura (ed.), *Matthew Arnold: A Collection of Critical Essays* (Prentice-Hall, Englewood Cliffs, 1973), pp. 15 - 23.
4. P. Brantlinger, *Bread and Circuses: Theories of Mass Culture as Social Decay* (Cornell University Press, Ithaca, 1983)
5. *Punch*, January 1985.
6. D. W. Brogan, 'The American Movies', in *American Themes* (Hamish Hamilton, London, 1948) 88 - 91 (88).

7. A. Visson, *As Others See Us* (Doubleday, New Jersey, 1948), p. 95.

8. UNESCO, *The Old World and the New World; Their Cultural and Moral Relations* (UNESCO, New York, 1954), p. 151.

9. Within three years, a number of seminal books taking this position were published: F. R. Leavis, *Mass Civilisation and Minority Culture* (1930); Ortega y Gasset, *The Revolt of the Masses* (1931); Karl Jaspers, *Man in the Modern Age* (1932); and Dover Wilson's new edition of Arnold's *Culture and Anarchy* (1932, the first new edition in 57 years). Cited in C. W. E. Bigsby, *Superculture: American Popular Culture and Europe* (Elek, London, 1975).

10. A. Lima in UNESCO, *The Old and the New World*, p. 86.

11. T. S. Eliot, 'Arnold and Pater', in DeLaura, *Matthew Arnold*, p. 10.

12. E. Goodheart, 'The Function of Matthew Arnold', *Critical Inquiry*, no. 9, (March, 1983).

13. D. H. Lawrence, *Architectural Review*, August, 1930.

14. Brantlinger, *Bread and Circuses*, p. 185.

15. Spengler, cited in Bigsby, *Superculture*, p. 8.

16. S. Lewis, *Babbitt* (Harcourt, Brace and Company, New York, 1922).

17. G. N. Shuster in UNESCO, *The Old and the New World*, p. 56.

18. F. R. Leavis and D. Thompson, *Culture and Environment* (Chatto and Windus, London, 1933), p. 3.

19. UNESCO, *The Old and the New World*, p. 151.

20. G. Orwell, 'The Lion and the Unicorn: socialism and the English genius' (Secker and Warburg, London, 1941) reprinted in *Collected Essays, Journalism and Letters of George Orwell*, (Penguin, London, 1970), vol. 2.

21. K. Fredriksson, '60 Years of American Rodeo in England, 1887 - 1947', *Brand Book*, no. 16, (1982).

22. W. Benjamin, 'The Work of Art in the Age of Mechanical Reproduction', in *Illuminations* (Schocken, New York, 1969).

23. This figure was widely cited in the 1920s and 1930s, perhaps most strongly in a memorandum from the association of Cinematograph Technicians to the Moyne Committee, 13 May 1936, PRO BT 55/3, C.C.F. 1.

24. Brogan, *American Themes*, p. 88.

25. Cited in J. Grierson, 'One Foot of Film Equals One Dollar of Trade', *Kine Weekly*, 8 January 1931.
26. *Kine Weekly*, 12 June 1930
27. Cited in H. Hopkins, *The New Look* (Secker and Warburg, London, 1963), p. 110.
28. R. Hewison, *In Anger: Culture in the Cold War, 1945-1960* (Weidenfeld and Nicolson, London, 1981), p. 2.
29. Leavis and Thompson, *Culture and Environment*, p. 100.
30. Q. D. Leavis, *Fiction and the Reading Public* (Russell and Russell, London, 1965, 1st edn 1932).
31. H. Hopkins, *England Is Rich : A Portrait at Mid-Century* (Harrap, London, 1957), p. 150.
32. G. Orwell, *The English People* (Collins, London, 1947), p. 36.
33. Hopkins, *England is Rich*, p. 32.
34. V. Zincone, 'Moral America', in J. Burnham (ed.), *What Europe Thinks of America* (John Day, New York, 1953), p. 40.
35. G. Hutton, *We Too Can Prosper,* (Allen and Unwin for the British Productivity Council, London, 1952).
36. J. J. Servan-Schreiber, *The American Challenge* (Atheneum, New York, 1968).
37. J. Ney, *The European Surrender: A Descriptive Study of the American Social and Economic Conquest* (Little, Brown and Co., Boston, 1970).
38. M. Abrams, *The Teenage Consumer* (London Press Exchange, London, 1959), p. 19.
39. R. Hoggart, *The Uses of Literacy* (Chatto and Windus, London, 1957); P. Willmott and M. Young, *Family and Kinship in East London* (Penguin, London, 1957).
40. T. Guback, *The International Film Industry: Western Europe and America Since 1945* (Indiana University Press, Bloomington, 1969).
41. G. H. Gallup (ed.), *The Gallup International Public Opinion Polls, Great Britain, 1937 - 1975,* (Random House, New York, 1976), Poll taken, March 1948.
42. *International Herald Tribune*, 10 April 1968.
43. H. J. Gans, American Films and Television Programs on British Screens: A Study of the Functions of American Popular Culture Abroad,, unpublished PhD dissertation,University of Pennsylvania, 1959.

Chapter Three

Three Pennyworth of Dark:
Postwar Deprivation in Britain and the Lure of the American Film

Britain historically has always been more vulnerable to American feature films than any other country, and until recently was Hollywood's most important overseas market. My central concern is to explain why British audiences expressed such a marked preference for the American feature film. Arguments based upon trade practices, government policies and other political/economic explanations do not really explain why British audiences expressed the preferences that they chose to at the cinema box office. The American feature film in Britain is an instance of overwhelmingly successful media colonialism. I have chosen for my time-frame the decade after the Second World War. This was a time when the British government pursued a very vigorous campaign against the American feature film. It is also the period when American popular culture in general was appropriated by Europeans.

As one cinemagoer wrote shortly after the war, in a reaction which, if perhaps excessive, was not altogether untypical of the time:

> My desire to go to the States had its origin in American
> films, But I am not fool enough to think that American life
> is just like Hollywood. What I do know is that everything
> American has an indescribable appeal to me. I like the
> American people, their idiom and way of life. I can tell by
> audience reactions that mine is not the normal British
> standpoint. Everybody likes American films, but with me,
> things British often irritate me, whereas for anything
> American I feel an unreasoned, impassioned loyalty such as
> one is usually supposed to have for the country of one's
> birth. [1]

Recent films like *A Private Function*, *Plenty* and even *Privates on*

Parade indicate a growing interest in the social and cultural changes which took place in Britain after the Second World War. These and also a number of recent books often take as their central theme the shabby and threadbare nature of life in postwar Britain. It is true that in 1946, and for several years afterwards, one could be forgiven for thinking, based upon the standard of living of the British people, that Britain had lost the war. For most people, acute shortages of food and fuel, of virtually all luxuries as well as many necessities were a feature of everyday life until the end of the decade. The dried egg crisis of 1946, the introduction of bread rationing later the same year, the snows, the floods and the droughts of 1947, all in hindsight seem to be a series of plagues visited upon the British after the war. In a situation curiously analogous to that of the Soviet economy today, people had purchasing power, but little to spend it on. The magazines of the time are full of advertisements promising items soon to be made available. The black marketeering and the fantasy of a nation freed from rationing and bureaucratic control presented so forcefully in *Passport to Pimlico* were firmly rooted in the realities of life in postwar Britain, for as one American magazine reported about life in Britain in 1948, 'Until recently, bananas, lemons, nylon stockings, potato chips, foreign travel for pleasure, a variety of sports equipment . . . were completely unavailable.' [2]

High taxes made those luxury items which were available increasingly expensive. The Labour government brought to an end for ever the period when beer and cigarettes were relatively inexpensive items in Britain. The cinema ranked alongside these as a heavily taxed luxury commodity, and a heavy entertainments tax, which typically took a larger share of the box office take than either the film producer or the distributor, was levied upon cinema admissions during and after the war. Meanwhile, even necessities were difficult to obtain in postwar Britain. Bread for example, which was never rationed during the war, became a rationed commodity in 1947. Clothes, meals in restaurants and coal were all tightly rationed until the end of the decade. There were perennial complaints that many items were actually harder to obtain in Britain than in Germany. As one writer in the *New Statesman* complained bitterly, 'At any medium priced restaurant in Munich you can eat better and more than in the best West End restaurants in London.' [3]

The cinema figured prominently in most people's lives as one of the few affordable luxuries which did not require a ration book. The authorities were very conscious of the manner in which films functioned as an important release from austerity, especially for the working class filmgoer. The British worker was on the front line in the export war and Hollywood regularly came up in discussions about schemes to maintain his, or more often her, morale and productivity. The major problem lay in the fact that films required spending precious dollars, and throughout the postwar decade there was a worldwide dollar famine. As one Treasury official noted at the time: 'If it were not for the dollar problem, films would be an enormous standby as giving the people something to spend their money on whilst production is still so far short of satisfying the needs of the home market.' [4] In the United States, it was widely understood that exports of films and tobacco compromised the benefits of any loans made to Britain by the United States. In May 1947, Billy Rose wrote: 'A recent statistic dramatizes what American flicks are doing to the British piggy bank. In the last six months of 1946, Yankee movies and tobacco took back $230 million of the first $600 million we advanced them on the Big Loan - almost 40%.' [5] Even ordinary citizens recognized that ultimately films were a major drain on precious dollars which could be used to purchase more nutritious fare. In 1946 when the *Daily Mirror* asked its readers to choose which dollar imports they would be willing to sacrifice first, the majority chose films, with tobacco, fruit and milk next on the list. [6]

The radical social and cultural consequences of the Second World War have recently received a great deal of serious scrutiny. [7] Perhaps the most significant broad social change was that Britain became a planned and bureaucratized society, in which class division played a far less significant role than it had before the war. The victory of the Labour Party in 1945 evidenced the extent of these sweeping changes, and in retrospect only the most blinkered observers could have been surprised by the extent of the Labour Party's victory. The belief that the war had been fought as much for social democracy as against Nazi Germany was shared by all levels of society. Consequently, after the war, the vocabulary of social democracy, previously anathema to Westminster and Whitehall, began to appear regularly in both government memoranda and newspaper headlines. Terms like 'the people', 'the masses' and other similarly egalitarian phrases were increasingly common in postwar Britain. This was very much in keeping with the manner in which postwar British governments were committed to a wide array of social as well as economic changes.

The massive bureaucracy created during the war survived into the peace and was in fact extended as the government expanded into new areas, assuming responsibility for many welfare programmes and a degree of control over industry previously inconceivable in peacetime. So much so that, by 1947, Conservative politicians were able to criticize the government for having three times as many civil servants as miners on the country's employment rolls. This produced a state which wove its way into virtually every aspect of daily life in Britain. Clement Attlee's government was committed to bringing the aspirations of the Beveridge plan, as well as its own socialist utopian ideas, into being. This, coupled to the difficulties of postwar reconstruction, was a major task. In its first nine months, the Labour government introduced 75 parliamentary bills, 55 receiving the royal assent, and this pace scarely slackened throughout the first Attlee administration. Coal, road haulage, the railways, the airlines: all were nationalized in quick succession. Housing estates and a national health service were set up. This rapid pace of reconstruction was necessary not only to fulfil the promises of the Labour Party's election manifesto, but also to recoup wartime losses. The growth of the role of the state in all aspects of everyday life affected everyone in postwar Britain.

The factor which overshadowed and often compromised many of these changes was that postwar Britain was immediately plunged into an intractable international trading situation. Through 1947 and 1948, for example, the United Kingdom participated in international trade at a monthly deficit of $280,000,000 (1948 dollars). Half of Britain's mercantile marine had been sunk, an even greater proportion of prewar investments had been sold off, and two-thirds of her prewar international trade had disappeared. Other possible sources of revenue, such as the royalties which ought to have accrued to British patents and inventions, had also been mortgaged. The terms of Lease-Lend and similarly the terms of the postwar Anglo-American loan were not generous and stretched Britain severely. Specifically, the United States had insisted on a return to full sterling-to-dollar convertibility within a year after the Anglo-American loan had been arranged . [8]

Britain embarked upon a postwar export drive, which was only possible at a price of a fairly hard life for most people. One sign of the times was the frequent use of billboard hoardings encouraging the British worker to 'work or want', a message which the average British worker was only too aware of, and yet did not want to hear, after so many years of hardship and deprivation. The stringencies of postwar food rationing were all too obvious at the time, as was the acute shortage of housing, clothing, furniture and, in fact, consumer items of any type. For example, in 1946, people who were eager to see new designs and the use of new materials developed during the war applied to less belligerent ends queued for hours to get into the 'Britain Can Make It' exhibit at the Victoria and Albert Museum. It was a sign of the times that most of the consumer items on display at the V . & A. were stamped 'Export Only', so that the popular press quickly renamed the show 'Britain Can't Have It'. There were many stories in the press at the time about the day-to-day grind of having to face shortages of all kinds. The Christmases of 1945 and 1946, for example, were marred by the absence of anything very much to serve as presents.

Siegfried Kracauer, writing about the representation of other countries and nationalities in Hollywood films, noted that the 'gloomy atmosphere' which he felt prevailed in Britain, and the 'socialist experiment' being conducted there had caused a dearth of Hollywood films set in Britain. After the war, just about the only American feature films in which Britain figured prominently were either historical subjects or films about the glories of the British Empire. The realities of postwar Britain were essentially invisible so far as Hollywood was concerned, except as a market. As Kracauer put it: 'Hollywood producers currently neglect, without perhaps consciously intending it, the living English in favour of their less problematic ancestors.' [9] Hollywood producers were very reluctant to give any serious attention to the changes taking place in Britain, but most off-putting for the studios, apart from successive trade disputes with the British government, was the pessimism and gloom which they felt shrouded shabby postwar Britain. Other factors such as the opposition of the many prominent film producers to British policies in Palestine were also significant in shaping American representations of postwar Britain.

The experiences of ordinary men and women living in Britain and the public lives and fictional lifestyles of the American stars most of them watched each week at the cinema were vastly different. It is perhaps hard to imagine the power which these illusions had over the cinema audiences of the period, and yet, pragmatically, there is no question that the cinema was a very important part of the everyday lives of the majority of the cinema audience.

1946 was the peak year for film-going in Britain. In the first full year of peace, cinema admissions totalled a record £121,000,000 (1946 prices). This was roughly equivalent to one-fifth of the nation's annual clothing bill, one-seventh of its yearly outlay on rent and light, or one-thirteenth of its expenditure on food. [10] Three years later, Britain's adult population still bought a total of 24,000,000 tickets each week, and had not begun to drift away from the box office as audiences already had in the United States. Cinema admissions inevitably tailed off from their wartime peak, but did not plummet as precipitately as they did in America. There were a number of surveys of the postwar British film audience, by the industry itself, and by ostensibly more neutral organizations like the Social Survey and the Hulton Research Organization. [11] One trade survey noted that for '40 % of the adult population, going to the movies is a regular item in the weekly schedule of relaxation'. At the same time, it also discovered that for 42% of the adult population, going to the cinema was a relatively rare event, whilst only 17% never went. [12]

There is no question that the cinema was the entertainment of choice for a very significant proportion of the British population. Certain classes and age groups were certainly markedly more faithful cinemagoers than others. Rachel Low thought the cinema audience consisted largely of habitual filmgoers for whom going to the cinema had become 'an institutionalized night out independent of the artistic value of the entertainment'. Examining the findings of the Social Survey, she discovered that fully 70% of the cinema-going public went exclusively to their 'local' cinema, making virtually no choice about which films they went to see. In other words, the experience of actually going to the cinema was, in her opinion, divorced for the most part from the artistic merits of individual films, and even perhaps their function as entertainment for 'most of these people are habitual filmgoers who exercise remarkably little choice between films'. She also noted the preponderance of the young amongst the most frequent cinemagoers. [13]

It is easy to cite figures for cinema audience size and composition, but it is much more difficult to assess the effect of the imaginary world into which people stepped after they had passed through the cinema lobby. Yet this is precisely what a number of studies undertaken by social scientists, government committees and a number of voluntary bodies attempted at the time, and this is also a very central concern of this work. Contemporary studies tended to be fixated with what they perceived as the adverse consequences of the American feature film, which in its most naive form sought to establish direct links between the popularity of American gangster films and the rising incidence of juvenile delinquency. Similarly, echoing the fears of earlier generations of moralizers, in the late 1940s, there were a number of studies of the effects of the cinema on children, which culminated in the report of the Wheare Committee. [14] The findings of these studies of the effects of the American feature film are a central concern of a later chapter. They evidence a concern for the manner in which the values of a very different culture were felt to be implanted into the minds of very suggestible cinemagoers of particular classes and ages.

The ruling Labour Party had a less obviously 'bread and circuses' approach to popular entertainment than the Conservative Party. Nevertheless, even they and their civil service advisors spoke largely in terms of maintaining 'industrial morale' when they discussed the impact of the American film on the British audience. For them, American feature films were seen very much as a necessary evil. Walter Fuller, head of the Cinematograph Exhibitors Association, attested to the importance of the American feature film as a palliative since he expected 'an even greater need in the difficult days approaching when the nation, instead of enjoying the fruits of its sacrifices, realizes that they have to be still further increased'. [15] Paul Addison has suggested that the Labour Party did not 'reflect on the influence of the American way of life' while it was in power and that 'Whether deep or shallow, the cultural influence of Hollywood was largely a matter of indifference to the Labour government.' [16] This view does not however, account for the *savoir-faire* shown by Gaitskell himself, by Harold Wilson and several other members of the Labour government in their dealings with the British film industry; they were acutely conscious of the threats, both cultural and economic, posed by the

American film industry in Britain.

Many of those who belonged to the traditional power elites, however, were apt to disparage Hollywood in much less equivocal terms. Feature films, like many other American imports, had historically been seen as harmful to the British Empire and to traditional social ties and other structures in Britain. In the 1920s, the effects of the American film upon the British Empire had frequently been discussed. The belief that 'trade follows the film, and not the flag' had empowered the initial attempts to legislate against the American film. The failure of this policy in the 1930s and some of its consequences both good (the British documentary movement) and bad (the infamous 'quota quickies') have been discussed elsewhere. [17] In the 1930s, some conservative groups found the general preference for American feature films inexplicable and, in a sense, disloyal. Drawing in part upon the prejudices discussed in an earlier chapter, they could not understand why most Britons expressed a preference for a culture so different from their own. Their position is best interpreted in the light of the very different class outlooks of Britain's working class, who went to the cinema regularly, and Britain's ruling elite, who did not. In fact, throughout the 1930s and 1940s, it was the cinema exhibitors who perhaps knew best what audiences wanted. Some of the most sophisticated entrepreneurs, like Sidney Bernstein, undertook their own public opinion polls. The Bernstein questionnaires are an important source of information about changing audience preferences over the course of more than a decade, and are particularly useful as an indicator of the changes which had taken place in the film audience during the war. [18] Such elaborate polls were rare, however, and most often exhibitors gauged audience tastes and reactions by overhearing the comments of patrons in the lobby after a performance, so that they were closer than any other members of the industry to the film audience, and were very conscious of audience preferences. However, exhibitors did not have a special interest in protecting and cultivating the production side of the British film industry. Until film exhibition, distribution and production were vertically integrated along American lines, the different branches of the British film industry had quite different vested interests. In particular, exhibitors were quite happy to show American films.

The 1927 and 1936 Cinematograph Films Acts were largely directed against renters and exhibitors. They tried to establish minimum quotas for British films rented and exhibited in Britain. The principal problem of this policy was that it encouraged British producers, but it paid no regard to the wishes of the British cinema audience. Not surprisingly then, the two prewar Cinematograph Films Acts did not revive British film production as had been hoped. By 1939, Britain had gone through a boom and bust cycle in the film industry and still produced only a fraction of the feature films which British cinema audiences saw each week.

During the war sophisticated polling and audience research techniques enabled policy makers and the film industry to gather much more detailed and accurate information about audience behaviour and preferences. The wartime expertise was appropriated by industry and government in peacetime and led to a series of studies of the British cinema audience.

Sidney Bernstein's Granada chain of cinemas had always had a tradition of keeping in touch with viewer preferences. The questionnaire which it circulated to its patrons in 1946 was the sixth such survey. It asked for detailed responses concerning viewers' preferences for particular genres, specific stars and specific films. Bernstein was particularly interested in the relative merits of British and American films and acting talent, and the questionnaire, returned when James Mason, Stewart Granger and Margaret Lockwood were the matinee idols of the day, evidenced surprising support for British films.

The J. Arthur Rank Organization, which had assumed the dominant position in the British film industry during the war, was equally anxious to research audience tastes in a scientific fashion. J. P. Mayer's classic two volume study of the British cinema audience, *The Sociology of Film* (1946), and *British Cinemas and Their Audiences* (1948), was begun initially under the auspices of the Rank Organization, although completed without its help. Mayer's work and the other studies are important sources for any investigation into the mentality of postwar British society and the postwar cinema audience. Mayer's own background was in political theory, and he had published widely on the work of de Tocqueville, the nineteenth century European commentator on American political institutions. De Tocqueville, and consequently Mayer himself, were very interested in the nature of American experiments in democracy, and this was at least partially the basis of Mayer's interest in the most democratic of art forms. He was also interested in the history of audiences for dramatic events. Although perhaps simplistic when judged in the light of contemporary techniques, his investigations into the nature of the viewing experience and the impact of film viewing upon social and psychological behaviour anticipated the current preoccupation in film studies with spectatorship, and with films and their reception. In his work on the postwar British cinema audience, Mayer employed a fairly straightforwardly ethnographic approach quite similar to that pioneered by the Mass Observation group in the 1930s. [19]

Mayer's principal source of information was a series of items placed in *Picturegoer*, the most popular film magazine of the time. Readers were asked to respond to a series of questions concerning their motion picture autobiographies, and small cash prizes were offered for the 'best' responses. Specifically, individuals were asked to trace their interest in films, and to try to suggest ways in which watching films had changed their behaviour. Had readers adopted mannerisms learnt from the screen? Had films inspired ambitions or shaped the personality traits of the reader? Using this outline questionnaire, Mayer solicited a self-selecting sample of audience responses, which provide a rare opportunity to hear the postwar cinema audience speaking for itself. [20]

Film viewers responding to Mayer's request commonly talked in the most general terms about the overall experience of going to the cinema, rather than the particulars of specific films. This was very much in keeping with the findings of the Social Survey, Hulton Research and other opinion polling organizations, which found that cinemagoers who went to see films regularly on the whole went to a specific local cinema, rather than making complex choices about seeing specific films. In the Mayer testimonies, some correspondents listed their preferences for particular films and specific stars, but generally this was not the main focus of their cinemagoing experiences. For the relatively unsophisticated cinemagoers who composed the majority of the postwar cinema audience in Britain, the formal and to a large extent the narrative elements of film were not the most important, central attributes of the film-viewing experience. Britain's postwar cinema audiences did not, as a rule, go to the cinema to make critical judgements about film art. People went to temporarily escape from the shortages, the queues, the rationing, the generally shabby nature of life in postwar Britain.

For many cinemagoers, and it is important to differentiate between the different elements within the audience, the film world spilled over into the real world of their lives outside the cinema. Mayer noted, for example, the manner in which films were an important, perhaps the most important, item of conversation amongst the young and the less well educated whilst at work or in leisure situations. His correspondents frequently referred to their preoccupation with the specifics of film storylines, the appearance of film stars, their clothing and their private lives. There is also some evidence that it was common for people to 'act out' situations which they had seen at the movies, which was support for the position of those who believed that films had a very adverse social effect upon the very susceptible audiences who went to see these films. As one of Mayer's testimonials noted:

> My sort of 'playing' was to act out in real life, either with my
> brother or with imaginary characters. I still talk to myself, and
> films have undoubtedly influenced me here because I always
> talk to myself in an American accent, and often think that way
> too. Most of the films I have seen were American because
> American films are the best. [21]

Typically this type of avid filmgoer went to the cinema twice a week and might spend five or six hours there, but would spend perhaps at least as long again each week reflecting in some way upon what he or she had seen there.

Similarly, the various popular film magazines devoted entirely, or in part, to the film industry had a vast circulation in the postwar decade. The paper shortage had led to the demise of many of the high brow small circulation journals of the time, like Cyril Connolly's *Horizon* which folded in 1949. In the postwar decade, popular newspapers and magazines, albeit generally small and printed on the poorest quality paper, enjoyed an unprecedented popularity, which in part attested to the growth of literacy - and the habit of reading - during the war. Hollywood was a staple subject for many magazines, especially those aimed at the female market. In the late 1940s, there were at least twenty-seven magazines devoted to films aimed at the general public, in addition to film journals for more specialized audiences. It was possible for a fan newsletter like the *International*

Jean Kent Fan Club Magazine to have a circulation rivalling that of the *Spectator*. The lay press also had cause to be grateful to the cinema audience, since, in a postwar survey, a majority of newspaper readers said that local film listings were the second most important reason for buying newspapers, whilst fully a fifth of the respondents in this survey said cinema listings were their most important reason for buying a newspaper. [22] In addition to the lay newspapers and popular magazines which incidentally covered the cinema, there was a whole genre of magazine devoted exclusively to the film industry and its stars, which will one day be the material for a whole thesis on the subject.

There were many visible 'spin-off' effects of films upon people's lives, which were sometimes directly a consequence of deliberate marketing and merchandizing campaigns, but often not. Fashions, in speech as well as dress, were the most conspicuous example of the impact of American feature films on the lives of British cinemagoers. Obviously, it is very difficult to isolate the impact of motion pictures from all the other avenues for American influences upon popular taste during the war and afterwards, and it is equally difficult to know how to quantify the extent to which changes in popular taste were being Americanized, or were evolving because of various other factors. Contemporary commentators, however, generally gave primary responsibility for these changes to Hollywood. As John Paddy Carstairs noted about this trend in July 1946, 'American clothes - "trick" clothes for the young men, snappy shoes for the young women, and so on, have become intensely popular over here, "glamourised", of course, by the Hollywood movie.' [23] It is significant that the notion of 'glamour' was sufficiently alien to a British writer to warrant quotation marks. Invariably it was believed that it was the younger cinemagoer who was most malleable. It was also generally assumed that it was Britain's least desirable and most immature citizens who were most anxious to be Americanized. Everybody was aware, for example, of the origins of the attire and demeanour of the stereotypical 'spiv' who was such a pervasive symbol of postwar British society. His clothing style, and some would say, his morality derived directly from the American gangster films of the 1930s.

Women were thought even more susceptible to the influence of motion pictures than men. In 1948 Hulton Research studied the extent to which British women used cosmetics. This is perhaps an area where it might be safe to assume popular preferences were based closely upon screen models. Whilst starting from the assumption that 'British women are not as beauty conscious as those in some other countries', the study found an astonishingly large - by prewar standards - number of women admitted that they made regular use of cosmetics. [24] Some studies maintained that the relatively youthful female cinema audience made disproportionate use of cosmetics, and this was certainly one of the findings of the Screen Advertising Association in a report written a decade later. By 1961, when people between the ages of 16 and 34 were found to constitute 60% of the cinema audience, the Screen Advertising Association maintained that cinemagoers were heavy consumers of cosmetics. [25]

In a similar vein, many of Mayer's correspondents, predominantly women, noted how they lusted after the clothing and consumer durables they saw in American films. One wrote that she would love to wear clothes like Lana Turner's and have an American-style white kitchen, if the Chancellor of the Exchequer would only let her. [26] The constant reiteration of visions of 'the good life' in American feature films, in the form of lavish meals and lavish settings was an important fuel for the emergence of a fully-fledged mass consumer society in Britain in the 1950s. In the 1940s, however, there were widespread reservations about the dangers which accompanied the lifestyle projected by American films. In 'Films and the idea of happiness', Gavin Lambert attempted to reconcile a British cinema whose best films were increasingly derivative of a fine art and very ascetic tradition and an American cinema which took a luxurious way of life very much for granted:

> recognising the condition of a society which finds that the few
> pleasures it can afford are nearly all restricted by the shortages.
> The tradition of good living . . . is not one ingrained in the
> British middle class, and when the hedonistic approach has to
> be cultivated, when society is not so organised to satisfy
> naturally the desire for good living, compensations are found
> remote from everyday life. In America, where material
> well-being is a determining social factor, good food, clothes,
> luxurious and elegant surroundings appear in every reasonably
> smart comedy and social drama. In Britain, the new and

remarkable popularity of ballet and 'good' music may in part be due to the food shortage, but it is mainly typical of people whose taste for everyday good living is largely undeveloped .. . To judge from the popular British cinema, the pursuit of luxury in everyday living is either criminal or disastrous. . . in *Good Time Girl* a nineteen-year-old bent on the pleasures of expensive clothes, food, wine and atmosphere, is quickly corrupted, indiscriminately seduced, and also lands in prison [27]

Writing in the mid-1950s, Harry Hopkins commented upon a type of social homogenization which went beyond mere appearance: 'The film, radio, and now television have made the same accent, manners and fashions accepted from Land's End to Berwick.' [28] There is also a lot of evidence that the manner in which people spoke was also very influenced by the adoption of the American idiom. Classless and regionless accents and vernacular crept into the English language during the postwar decade. The BBC deserves little credit for postwar changes in the English language, since it continued to encourage a 'BBC' accent, an exaggerated amalgam of Oxbridge, minor public school and the home counties, which did not acquire a large following. Nevertheless, the BBC accent was adulterated somewhat by the deliberate cultivation of self-consciously 'regional' accents, like that of Wilfred Pickles. However, Pickles was very much in the North of England 'just plain folks' tradition of Formby and Fields, and his idiomatic North of England expressions and manner did not enter into mainstream vernacular to anything like the extent of many expressions from the other side of the Atlantic.

The principal school for the new idiom was the cinema. The English working class had by the 1940s learnt the necessity of using different 'languages' in different contexts. As Winifred Holtby had noted in *South Riding* a decade earlier, 'Like most of her generation and locality, Elsie was trilingual. She talked BBC English to her employer, Cinema American to her companions, and Yorkshire dialect to old milkmen like Eli Dickson.' [29] Perhaps the most significant development after the war was the extent to which generation differences were increasingly significant in shaping the way in which people spoke. Teenagers after the war not only looked and dressed differently, but they had a separate vocabulary and idiom too.

After the war, it was very difficult for English people to travel overseas unless they were in the armed forces. The Hulton Survey found that in 1947, only 3.3% of the total adult population of Britain spent their holidays abroad, and in fact fully 43% did not take a vacation of any kind. [30] The movies were the only chance most people had to 'visit' overseas and the country they saw most often in their travels was the United States. As one of Mayer's correspondents noted:

> From an early age I have been imbued with an intense
> admiration for America and most things American. The films I
> have seen have increased this. Whilst at school, which I left
> when I was sixteen, I used as many American slang phrases as
> I could, and put up with being laughed at by my school
> companions - who were, as most English schoolgirls are, just
> content to follow each other, and ready to make fun of any
> original ideas, being quite content to stay in their own familiar
> rut. Nowadays everyone uses American slang, but when I did it
> five years ago, it was quite a brave thing to do. [31]

It is very hard to gauge the impact of the images of American society which permeated the imaginations of British cinemagoers. In a recent text, Paul Addison uses oral testimony to illustrate the 'magical power' exercised by images of America in austerity Britain. As one of his witnesses noted, 'America, at the time, seemed to be a land of everything, you know, a land of milk and honey, where there's us poor little English people, or British people, had virtually nothing'. [32] It seems likely that such sentiments were very widely held, and this must be considered as part of the context for the consumer society into which Britain developed in the 1950s. Certainly, examples of idealized images of the United States - 'drug stores', 'college campuses' and the like - abounded in British cinemagoers' comments on their experiences at the cinema. The remarks of J.P. Mayer's respondents imply that many were aware that things in America were not necessarily exactly like what they saw at the cinema, but that for them it was hard to differentiate between truth and mediated artifice.

There is a lot of evidence to imply that for some cinemagoers, what they saw at the cinema was actually 'more real' than their own lives. It is easy to speculate on the literally 'larger than life' aspects of going to the cinema, especially since the disparity between life projected inside

45

the cinema and experienced outside it was so great. For example, many testimonies noted how they were 'in love' with this or that cinema star - and this was not limited to American stars. Postwar Britain had a whole generation of leading men who were the subject of adoration for large followings. The nature of the star/fan relationship will be explored in greater detail in a later chapter. 'Fans' did not make up the majority of the film audience and their behaviour ought not be regarded as typical. Nevertheless, they were an extreme by-product of the process of cross-cultural transmission between Great Britain and the United States.

Film producers and the manufacturers of luxury consumer items were very conscious of the power which films exerted over their viewers. There was a strange irony about a situation where everybody was convinced about the merchandising potential of motion pictures, including an audience which was anxious to consume commodities denied to them during the war, and yet there was little enough of anything to be consumed. At a time when clothing was strictly rationed, so much so that the difficulties of obtaining sufficient clothing coupons to equip Britain's international cross-country team became a national problem, terms like 'luxury' were completely relative. [33] Mark Abrams' Research Services Company studied the prospects of using films to market other items. It produced a number of reports for the Rank Organization, and drew heavily upon the material gathered by the Hulton Surveys. Abrams noted the extent to which the cinema audience was drawn heavily from the poorer and younger parts of the general population. He wrote in an article for *Hollywood Reporter*, 'The Working Classes flock to the movies with such avidity that they account for more than 70% of the audience.' [34] There are many competing estimates about the demographics of the postwar cinema audience in Britain, but all suggest this sort of class bias.

It is interesting to note the subsequent development of Abrams' social research, which spanned more than a decade after the war; it concluded in the late 1950s with a report on teenage consumer preferences, which in many respects was the inevitable consequence of regarding the film audience primarily as a group of highly suggestible consumers. The 1961 Screen Advertising Association's *The Screen Audience: A National Survey* which aimed to 'sell' the film audience as consumers to potential advertisers, was the logical conclusion of this process. In the earlier studies, Abrams identified significant differences in the behaviour of the cinema audience. For example, he maintained that typical female filmgoers were much more likely to wear make-up than their contemporaries, whilst men who went regularly were much more likely to gamble than those who did not. In other words, behaviour and habits which had been regarded as anti-social in previous eras were now regarded as something to be exploited by the retailer. Obviously, it is very difficult to separate the general social behaviour of those classes and groups who went to the cinema most frequently from specific social habits connected with their cinemagoing. Did people who went to the cinema have these characteristics because they they went to the cinema, or because they were young and for the first time had a significant disposable income of their own? It is equally difficult to identify any direct causal relationships between cinemagoing and the acquisition of new mannerisms and fashions. What is perhaps most significant is that the trade was so interested in analysing the viewer, its willingness to think of viewers primarily as the consumers of material commodities, and the many attempts made at the time to identify patterns linking the motion picture to emerging consumerism.

For very pragmatic reasons, advertisers and the film trade were aware of the extent to which, for over twenty years, films had been encouraging film audiences to behave in specific ways. After the war, British cinemagoers had to defer gratifying their own material hopes until Britain's economic recovery was under way. Like virtually all British people, they had no choice in the matter. However, they were able to satisfy their appetites in a sublimated way by consuming images, if not the goods themselves, in the films which emanated from the United States.

Notes

1. Document # 1, J. P. Mayer, *British Cinemas and their Audiences* (Dennis Dobson, London, 1948).
2. A. Dawson, 'British and American Motion Picture Wage Rates Compared', *Hollywood Quarterly*, vol. 3, no. 3 (1948).

3. R. Hewison, *In Anger : Culture in the Cold War, 1945-1960* (Weidenfeld and Nicolson, London, 1981), p. 18.
4. E. Rowe Dutton to H. M. Nicholson, March 1947, PRO BT 64/2283.
5. B. Rose, Pitching Horseshoes, Bell Syndicate Press Release, May 1947, Lincoln Centre for the Performing Arts.
6. S. Cooper, 'Snoek Piquante', in M. Sissons and P. French (eds.), *The Age of Austerity* (Penguin, London, 1964), p. 39.
7. A. Marwick, *British Society Since 1945* (Allen Lane, London, 1982), P. Addison, *Now the War is Over* (Jonathon Cape, London, 1985).
8. For a full account of the loan from an individual intimately involved in the negotiations, see R. Clarke, *Anglo-American Economic Co-Operation in War and Peace, 1942 - 1947* (Clarendon Press, Oxford, 1982).
9. S. Kracauer, 'National Types as Hollywood Sees Them', *Public Opinion Quarterly*, no. 13 (1949), pp. 53-72.
10. M. Abrams, 'The British Cinema Audience', *Hollywood Quarterly*, vol. 3, no. 2, (1947-8), pp. 155-8.
11. See Hulton Research, *Patterns of British Life* (Hulton, London, 1948).
12. M Abrams, 'The British Cinema Audience, 1949,' *Hollywood Quarterly*, vol. 4, no. 3 (1950), p. 252.
13. R. Low, The Implications Behind the Social Survey', in R. Manvell (ed.),*The Penguin Film Review*, 7, (Penguin, London, 1948).
14. There was a series of studies of children's film viewing habits in the late 1940s, culminating in the Social Survey's *Children and the Cinema* (Central Office of Information, London, 1948) and the *Report of the Departmental Committee on Children and the Cinema* (HMSO, London, 1950). There were also many popular articles dealing with the same issue, e.g. G. Greiner, 'Children and the Cinema', *Christus Rex*, July 1954, pp. 252-260, as well as responses by the industry such the Motion Picture Association of America and British Film Producers Association's *Delinquent Children .. A World Problem* (MPEA, New York, 1950).
15. W. R. Fuller to C. M. Attlee, 12 August 1947, PRO BT 64/2283
16. Addison, *Now the War is Over*, pp. 133, 200-1.

17. See P. Swann, 'The Empire Marketing Board and Imperial Film Propaganda', in *Studies in Visual Communication*, September 1983, for a study of the ties between official film production and the notion that American feature films threatened the British Empire. See also S. Street and M. Dickinson, *Cinema and State* (British Film Institute, London, 1985), Ch. 1.
18. *Bernstein Film Questionnaire, 1946-1947*. This was the sixth questionnaire, distributed between December 2 and December 31, 1946.
19. For a discussion of Mass Observation's work with film, see T. Harrisson, 'Films and the Home Front - the Evaluation of Their Effectiveness by "Mass Observation"', in N. Pronay and D.W. Spring(eds.), *Propaganda, Politics and Film, 1918-1945* (Macmillan, London, 1982). Mass Observation also produced a number of studies of audience reactions to specific British films after the Second World War, see 'Film and Public: Chance of a Lifetime', *Sight and Sound*, vol. 19, no. 9, (1951), pp. 349-50.
20. Mayer's initial call for responses was listed in the *Picturegoer*, February 1945:

Your Help Is Requested

  A Lecturer at the University of London has asked for your assistance. He is conducting an investigation regarding film audiences. He would like to ask you two questions:
  1. Have films ever influenced you with regard to personal decisions or behaviour (love, divorce, manners, fashion, etc). Can you give instances?
  2. Have films ever appeared in your dreams?
  You may write to your heart's content. There is no limit to wordage and the best will be rewarded by a guinea, 10 shillings and two prizes of five shillings.

21. Mayer, *British Cinemas and their Audiences*, document # 2.
22. L. England, 'What The Cinema Means To The British Public', *The Year's Work in the Film*, 1949.
23. J.P. Carstairs, 'All This and Export Too', *Film Industry: Monthly Review of Film Production*, vol. 1, no. 1 (1946), p. 4.
24. Hulton Research, *Patterns of British Life*, p. 60.

25. Screen Advertising Association, *Spotlight on the Cinema Audience: A National Survey* (SCA, London, 1961), p. 22.
26. Mayer, *British Cinemas and their Audiences*, document # 8.
27. G. Lambert, 'Films and the Idea of Happiness', *Good Living* (1948), pp. 61-5.
28. H. Hopkins, *England is Rich : A Portrait at Mid-Century* (Harrap, London, 1957), p. 150.
29. W. Holtby, *South Riding* (Macmillan, New York, 1936).
30. Hulton Research, *Patterns of British Life*, p. 114.
31. Mayer, *British Cinemas and their Audiences*, document # 58.
32. Addison, *Now the War is Over*, p. 201.
33. Cooper, 'Snoek Piquante', p. 37.
34. Abrams, 'The British Cinema Audience', *Hollywood Quarterly*, vol. 3, no. 2 (1947-8).

Chapter Four

Selling the American Way:
The Ideology of the American Motion Picture

> British working class culture is rather more hospitable than
> middle class culture to the violent and the cynical, with the
> result that American movies sometimes come much nearer the
> actual attitudes of British audiences than most British ones. [1]

> Persistently and adroitly, we must make the foreign movie-goer
> acutely conscious that the American picture is a product of
> decidedly superior quality - of rich and varied artistry, of
> entertainment value unmatchable in the run-of-time output of
> our competitors abroad. We must make this 'High Quality'
> factor so universally recognised that local audiences abroad will
> have no desire to see inferior films that owe their existence
> simply to some Government legislation or subsidy. [2]

The two major approaches which dominate the study of film and
film history could be said to revolve broadly around the general areas of
cinema as art and as social institution. The film-as-art approach focuses
on the visual aspects of cinema, specifically film as form. It is
concerned with visually coding films, and attempts to explain, interpret
and order the visual conventions or codes which have come to govern
narrative film form and structure. These codes may be straightforward
visual ones, such as iconography, editing, the work of a particular
director, a specific studio, historical period, and specific production
contexts.

Many social and sociological perspectives on cinema are interested
in assessing the impact of film upon society and also the manner in
which the collective values and ideology of a society become encoded
in its cultural forms. In the 1930s and 1940s, this type of approach
was often closely tied to the market research and audience surveys
conducted by the industry itself, and was consequnetly rarely critical in

any direct way. The industry supported a number of behavioural studies of the cinema audience, interested in marketing and in controlling any attempts to regulate the content of its output. Perhaps the most interesting of these was the Motion Picture Association of America's efforts to undermine any attempts to associate the motion picture with juvenile delinquency and harm to the sociological and pyschological well-being of children, with a series of reports culminating in *Juvenile Delinquency . . . A World Problem,* in which eminent behaviour specialists like Sir Cyril Burt denied any direct links between behaviour and motion pictures. [3]

This work is primarily interested in those studies which have examined the motion picture as a vehicle for the transmission of cultural values. In the last fifteen years, a relatively impartial academic discipline has emerged, only obliquely linked to the direct interests of the industry. For example, Norman L. Friedman, drawing on the work of Robin Williams, has discussed the way in which the motion picture has served as a conserving agent of cultural transmission and as an agent of cultural innovation. These are the values which Robin Williams has suggested are central to postwar American society:

1. Achievement values: activity, work, accomplishment, success.
2. Material and rational values: material comfort and progress; efficiency and practicality; science and secular rationales.
3. Humane values: humanitarianism, freedom, equality; ethical universalism; moral orientation.
4. Miscellaneous values: conformity, nationalism; democracy; racial or group superiority; value of the individual. [4]

There are also some approaches, specifically structuralism, which offer the prospect of combining the considerations of film structure and design with the central concerns of a society producing and consuming motion pictures. Drawing on the work of Levi-Strauss and the Russian formalists, Will Wright and others have used the notion of myth to explain the shape, form and, most importantly perhaps, the function of the American genre film. [5] Cine-structuralists are interested in the essentially compulsive and ritualistic aspects of recurrent story-telling which are a very central element of the American feature film. They stress the essentially explanatory nature of narratives of all kinds.

What were the central myths of American feature films in the 1940s and 1950s? It is important to ascertain which values were reiterated coherently and repeatedly in Hollywood's exports, and the extent to which they worked in a similarly mythic way for people in other countries and contexts. One essential attribute of myth is its universality - but myth is also culture and context specific. It is only universal in the extent to which it is shared by a group with a consensus about a specific myth. The issue therefore becomes the extent to which myth is transportable - or whether this kind of transmission produces new myths.

There were a number of studies in the postwar years into the sort of values and type of impact which American motion pictures were felt to promote, especially from the domains of sociology and pyschology. These provide a strong indication of what the Establishment thought were the views and values promoted by the American motion picture. As Andre Visson noted: 'Clippings from the American and foreign press attacking Hollywood for its pernicious influence, and for the harm it has done to American prestige abroad, would fill the shelves of a very impressive library.' [6]

On the British side of the Atlantic, attributes such as shallow emotions, hedonism, crass commercialism and violence ranked near the top of most critics' lists of the endemic attributes of the American feature film. In a fairly straightforward behavioural way, pyscho -logists, sociologists and politicians associated Hollywood with a cluster of emotions and character traits felt to have an adverse effect on the more impressionable cinemagoers. This guilt by association did little to improve the image of the United States in Europe. It was so widely accepted that motion pictures were harmful that the only real point at issue seemed to be the extent to which it was felt these qualities were being indoctrinated into cinemagoers, or merely bringing out traits that were already there. As the *Documentary News Letter* noted:

American feature films are building up a conception of America
in the minds of the European public which is false and
damaging. Is it to be wondered that many British cinema-goers
see America as a place of luxury and shallow sentiment?..they
represent a sickly-sweet commodity prepared solely for
commercial profit, and with an irresponsible lack of attention to

the deeper pyschological values. [7]

In Britain, pyschologists and social scientists had begun assessing the impact of the American feature film during the 1920s. Reports such as *The Film in National Life* were all a consequence of this concern for the effects of the American feature film on the British people. After the Second World War, the same experts focused more narrowly upon a range of issues and problems which were thought to be imported along with G.I.s and films. Invariably, they felt that the young were much more vulnerable to the effects of the motion picture than were any other group:

> Much has been written and said about the effect of cinema attendance on the behaviour patterns of children and adolescents. It has been suggested that delinquency and crime have been inspired by incidents presented on the screen, that techniques of behaviour, ways of amusement, speech, manners, and, in fact, almost every department of behaviour are being permeated by influences from the cinema. On the other hand there have not been lacking authorities who contend that, if it does anything at all, the screen merely provides the form in which impulses already present declare themselves. [8]

These Cheap and Nasty Films

Was it any surprise that there were recurrent attempts to stem the flow of 'cheap and nasty' films from the United States in the House of Commons? [9] Financial motives always underlay the House's concern, but value judgements about 'the American Way of Life' (an increasingly common phrase) were frequent in House debates about American films. This is what Richard Adams thought about the effects of the American motion picture in Britain:

> I feel that we are in danger in this country of coming far too much under the influence of American civilisation. When we consider that the cinema is indirectly a form of propaganda, we must appreciate how significant it is that, every week, millions of the public go and sit for several hours in a cinema and come under the influence of American opinion and the American way of life. According to the films, the American either lives in a vast house, much larger than the Savoy or Dorchester, and

much more ornately furnished, or else he lives in slums far worse than anything we have in England, and walks about habitually carrying a sub-machinegun. [10]

In America, there was a similar interest in the way in which Hollywood was felt to proselytize for an 'American way'. Motion Picture Export Association President Eric Johnston, for example, regarded American films overseas as 'messages from the free country'.[11] Most American commentators regarded the culture emanating from other countries as propaganda, but saw their own output as true and fair representation. Walter Wanger, for example, wrote in an article for *Public Opinion Quarterly* in 1950:

> The motion picture industry has been the nearest thing to Senator Benson's conception of a Marshall Plan for Ideas . . . Strangely enough, we have never been nationalistic. No one has ever been able to say that Hollywood did not want talent because it was English, French, Italian, German or Russian. There has never been any nationalistic thinking on subjects or castings, and our pictures are still the most popular in the world. We have more international content in our pictures than is to be found in the films of any other country. We have large groups of foreign experts who watch our productions in preparation and in production and then check them when completed to see that nothing in them will offend foreign nations when the films are circulated abroad. We maintain a huge distribution organization throughout the world, manned by experts who watch the reactions to our films daily, who see how the people respond to the features and the newsreels. They know what the audiences applaud and what they boo. We have a greater check on the latest reactions throughout the world, I venture to say, than does the State Department, and I am sure we have a larger staff. Thus, every important distributor receives a constant flow of reports which reflect current attitudes in dozens of countries. [12]

He saw nothing essentially colonial in the way in which Hollywood appropriated the best European talent for itself, nor any unfairness in the essentially monopolistic nature of Hollywood's marketing strategies overseas.

A number of recent studies have attempted to link specific American film genres and even individual films to the institutional settings in which they were produced. Such work generally foregrounds the role of the studio production context, maintaining that the industrial and commodity nature of Hollywood's output have made it very prone to functioning as a principal vehicle for ideology. For example, Nick Roddick's recent study of Warner Brothers examines that studio's output as an extension of the New Deal, and Brian Henderson's recent article on the production context for *Flying Down To Rio* relates that film to the industrial conglomerate which both produced the film and was also developing civil aviation. [13] Along similar lines is recent work by Peter Biskind and Richard Maltby, both of whom are essentially interested in the notion of social consensus as the central governing ideology in the American genre film. Biskind uses this approach in *Seeing Is Believing* to suggest how the fifties *Zeitgeist* was inscribed upon the vast majority of genre films produced during that time to create a very consistent stating and restating of a specific ideological position and set of values. Biskind's valuable contribution is a way of reading films produced in Hollywood in the forties and fifties which permits one to see widely disparate genre films subscribing essentially to the same position. [14] The fifties can be viewed as the period when Americans faced, but did not resolve, the essential contradictions between the American traditions of individualism and conformity. In many forms of popular culture, as Biskind argues in the case of the feature film, one partial resolution was acheived by producing films which were about the necessity of creating and controlling consensus, whether by the left, the centre or the right.

The search for consensus became all the more highlighted because there was a far greater diversity of films than there had been in the 1930s, and the range of opinions they expressed seems no less heterogeneous. For example, there was some revision in the way in which 'the American way of life' was represented on film. Elsewhere, it has already been suggested that, in Europe at any rate, this 'way of life' was synonymous with a fairly broad but essentially naive and juvenile range of emotions and positions, revolving around the peaks and troughs of melodramatic forms. Even recently the appeal of American popular culture in Europe was interpreted using this approach. As Raymond Durgnat commented, 'For some English and

European intellectuals, American cliches possess the double appeal of a) a hard-edged dynamism, and b) the spurious and specious exoticism of scarcely nuanced emotional and moral primitivism.' [15] In the postwar years the American film industry had a rather more positive, if simplistic, view of the appeal of their products in postwar Europe:

> There is something vital and gay in the American people
> which comes over in so many of their films...Their love of
> dancing, jiving and outdoor sports of all kinds is proof of this.
> In a Europe that is tired and weary and in many parts unable or
> unwilling to help itself, this transatlantic vitality mirrored in
> the film offers some sort of dream hope. Peace-weary citizens
> visit their cinemas and for a few hours are able to forget the
> taut, unhappy faces in the queues and assorted ill-tempered
> officials and sink into a world that is 100% living - where
> people in fact live life, not just endure it. [16]

What constituted the 'American way of life' for a European film audience was not synonymous with what that term connotated for the American film audience. In the United States, this mythic way of life resided in Edwardian, midwestern, smalltown America as exemplified in the *Andy Hardy* series and *Meet Me In St Louis*. After the war, this vision of a largely imaginary and historically remote America continued to be articulated and sometimes updated in films like *Cheaper by the Dozen* and *Father of the Bride*. For some British cinemagoers also, this transparent representation of a mythic America was very real. As one of J. P. Mayer's correspondents noted: 'I think that Mickey Rooney and Judy Garland, and Cecilia Parker and the rest of the "Hardy Family" are as true to life as possible in a film.' [17] Only a small number of British films retailed similarly idealistic views of cosy British family life. In Britain, *The Huggetts* series was one of the few sustained attempts to portray family life in film on a regular basis. In addition, in the Ealing films made in this period there was also the message of community, but this message was rarely restricted to within the single family as was generally the case in the American films. As Charles Barr has noted, a handful of Ealing comedies espoused a very powerful 'little England' mentality which was very much in keeping with the community nature of the Ealing studio itself. [18] Interestingly, there were plenty of films made in Britain towards the end of the war about stylized utopias in the future -

films like *They Came to a City*, *The Canterbury Tale* and *A Matter of Life and Death* were very self-conscious and mannered attempts to indicate what society in the world of tomorrow would be like in Britain.

In postwar Hollywood, there was a growing critique of the midwestern-based 'American way', as evidenced in films like *My Son John* and *Picnic*, which all emphasised the possibilities for betrayal and duplicity in the traditional American family. The American family and community now harboured something potentially malicious in their midst. A close relative might be a murderer or, even worse, a communist. In films like *Picnic*, interlopers were always presented as a threat to the integrity and safety of the family. In general, Hollywood films were much more morally and socially ambiguous than they had been before the war. Many films, like *The Man in the Grey Flannel Suit*, characterized ordinary people - the 'lonely crowds' of the popular sociology books of this period - as leading lives of 'quiet desperation'.[19] In one way, this was a representation of an increasingly malleable perception of a social reality; in another, it was tied to the changing circumstances of Hollywood production itself.

The old-style studio system broke down in the 1950s. By the mid-1950s, the majority of films were being produced by independent producers, not the studios themselves. Many independently produced films, like *High Noon*, mirrored their production context. Independent producers used the studios essentially as production facilities, and did not have to subscribe to studio aesthetic and studio orthodoxy in quite the way their predecessors had. They were much more likely to produce films which did not have such a broad and uplifting appeal, although Biskind argues that all mainstream American films from this period retailed the same ideology. For Biskind, all Hollywood films in the fifties were 'about' consensus, and films of different political persuasions attempted to persuade the viewer that consensus ought to be under the control of the right, the left, or the centre. *On the Town*, according to this view, sold the same position to the cinema audience as *On the Waterfront*. The Ben Hecht-Burt Lancaster 1957 production, *The Sweet Smell of Success*, was perhaps the paradigm of the new sobriety in American film. The film's very pessimistic vision of journalism and especially the cynical and self-serving actions of a columnist who is 'the choice of fifty million Americans' was very much in contrast to the traditional escapism of the American feature film. The film is equally bleak in showing the dark side of upward social mobility and the harsh rewards of social climbing.

Genre Film in the Fifties

Film genres such as the western and the musical, which had perhaps been the purest objectifications of the American way, if not in their representation of family life, then at least in their unbounded energy and optimism, had an increasing element of self-doubt about them. Genre has been at the heart of much that has been written in the area of film theory in the last decade. It has provided theorists with an opportunity to examine the American film as collective myth/coherent fantasy. It is a useful way of looking at how the industrial mechanism of Hollywood and the American psyche, mediated at the Box Office intertwine. Consequently, Will Wright and Jane Feuer have used the notion of genre as a means of discussing the function of Hollywood film as myth. [20]

The western myth has its own history, and Wright has charted its shift from the classical, idealist western of the thirties and forties, via revenge films made in the fifties, to professional/corporate films made in the sixties and seventies. He attempts to link these shifts to current social changes. Jane Feuer's analysis of the musical, is much less historically specific, and is much more a commentary upon the myths associated with heterosexual romance and entertainment itself. Significantly, both genres in the early fifties were full of self-doubt and self-questioning. This can be linked to the growing cynicism of the industry as whole, increasingly beset by financial problems and competition with television. *High Noon* and *It's Always Fair Weather* were paradigms of the new cynicism. *High Noon* is a western where the hero has to fight both the villain and the frontier community he traditionally protected. This was a radical revision of the classical western's straightforward conflicts between good and evil.

It's Always Fair Weather, a fairly typical musical from the mid-fifties, is a particularly sombre musical which exemplifies the end to the era of effervescent MGM/Gene Kelly musicals . Like *The Bandwagon*, it attempted to repeat the formula of these earlier musicals but without success. It, and most of the other musicals produced at this time were increasingly self-conscious about their origins and their intentions. Consequently, both films are about show business. Both *High Noon* and *It's Always Fair Weather* were eulogies to the genre film and the ageing of the industry which had created them. Both, in common with an increasing number of musicals and westerns at this time were films about genre, not straightforward genre films themselves.

There have been a number of sustained analyses of the manner in which 'adult' themes came to pervade American films made in the late forties and early fifties, and the increasing self-consciousness of the genre film was tied to this. What this fails to explain is the growing pessimism associated with the postwar American film. The war itself, the atomic bomb and the onset of the Cold War were all parts of this historical matrix. It was perhaps not surprising that although the influence of the Second World War pervaded many postwar American films, the war itself quickly fell out of favor as a subject for films. Interestingly enough, this was not the case in Britain. There, the prisoner of war film was emerging as a sub-genre film in its own right. The Korean conflict produced a spate of combat and 'home front' films, but the issues and sides were rarely as clear cut and clearly defined as they were in films which dealt with the Second World War. Perhaps this was a consequence of changes in the market place as much as anything - the film audience in the early 1950s was younger and much less family-centred than that a decade earlier. Also, in the United States, at any rate, if people wanted to see the Korean war, they could see it at home. The Korean war has the distinction of being the first 'televised' war, and Edward R. Murrow's reports from the Korean front anticipated by over a decade the capability of making war real to civilians which television demonstrated so fully during the Vietnam conflict.

The America of *The Best Years of Our Lives* was at best only barely recognisable in *Invasion of The Body Snatchers*. It is possible to see how the images and sensibilities of the first film gradually shaded into the persecution complexes and suspicions of the latter film. This is to talk in terms of extremes: most films made during the postwar decade occupied the middle ground. American society, even when repressed and undermined was invariably re-presented as wealthy, orderly and egalitarian. Prewar habits died hard and those films which suggested a less than clear-cut vision of how America saw itself, such as the image of midwestern America in *Picnic*, or corporate America in

Executive Suite, were the exceptions rather than the rule. The ethos of materialism was rarely challenged, even in these films, although American films also generally criticized excessive wealth and avarice. As Gavin Lambert noted at the time:

> Innumerable scenes in Hollywood films take place over an excellent meal, rounded off with coffee: even what the characters like for breakfast, what they drink habitually, may be important. The average American production takes for granted the fact of good food, coffee, efficient bars, clothes, apartments" [21]

At the same time, Lambert was very conscious of the strong puritanical streak in many American films, like *Citizen Kane* and *Mr Deeds Goes to Town*, which suggested that 'wealth and luxury in extremis are corrupting factors, and go hand in hand with ruthless, dishonest big business methods'.

Britain

> Films should be the bagmen not only of our commerce but of our ideas, to show abroad our way of life; and also, no less important, to interpret our own culture and our own way of life to our own young cinema going public here. [22]

Britain figured prominently in films made in Hollywood before and during the war. There were so many expatriate British actors in Hollywood - a situation satirized by Evelyn Waugh, after a visit to California, in *The Loved One* - that American producers could field an entirely British cast when making a Hollywood film depicting Britain. Hitchcock's *Rebecca* and Lubitsch's *Cluny Brown* are both good examples of this. The Britain represented in these films tended to be either safely historical like the Warner Brothers' historical epics, literary and mythical as in *Pride and Prejudice,* or the very idealized Britain of *How Green Was My Valley* and *National Velvet*. The British Empire was also frequently romanticized in many American films made during this period.

Representatives of contemporary Britain and British life were conspicuously absent from Hollywood fs made in the immediate postwar years, which is perhaps surprising in view of the importance of the British market for the American film industry. Siegfried

Kracauer attributed this to Hollywood's hostility towards the British Labour government and its development of the welfare state, noting, 'what is now going on in Britain means a challenge to the American belief in free enterprise'; although he did agree that 'the gloomy aspect of life in Britain, hardly attractive to a screen infatuated with glamour' was also a factor. [23] In the 1950s, this changed when American companies made more films in Britain than in the previous decade in order to use the funds they had frozen there and to escape higher production costs back home. Films like *The Million Pound Banknote* tried to graft the ambitions and aspirations of the American feature film on to the British period film. Nevertheless, throughout the decade, British audiences saw much more of American society on their cinema screens than they saw of their own.

During the American film embargo *The Times* took a break from reporting nothing but dire news about the mounting financial crisis and instead took the opportunity to comment humorously upon the image of Britain represented in American films. An editorial entitled 'England, their England' noted that, as the time approached when there would be no more American films in Britain, Britain would probably be able to remedy the shortage of most film genres:

> Neither our climate nor the mouths of our horses are particularly well adapted to the making of 'westerns', but there is no reason why we should not have a shot at it. As for tremendously bad films about the lives of celebrated composers, we can turn them out at a pinch. . . no amount of ingenuity can ever provide a substitute, only one loss which we must steel ourselves to writing off as irrecoverable and that is the Hollywood version of life in Great Britain . . . a quaint, dreamlike charm all of its own . . . wrapped almost all the year round in a dense fog...Its aristocracy were, though not particularly powerful, numerous and, though stupid, generally condescending; they often had beautiful American daughters . . . The lower orders, a cheerful lot, wore gaiters in the country, but in London, being mostly costers, dressed in a manner which befitted this calling . . . But it was a wonderful place, and the only general criticism which can be levelled at the inhabitants is that when, as frequently happened, they met an American they betrayed an almost complete lack of understanding of the American way of life. [24]

In the mid-1950s, Herbert Gans, then a young researcher at the School of Urban Planning at the University of Pennsylvania, travelled to Britain to study the impact of American films and television programmes on British audiences. His main thesis was that Hollywood films had attractions for British audiences which their own films lacked. In particular, he argued that a predominantly young and working class audience was to a large extent alienated by/from the middle class, middle-aged image of British society retailed by most British feature films. At the same time, this same audience was attracted to Hollywood films which gave them 'aspiration fantasies' and fulfilled them on the screen. American films offered tales of material gain and social mobility and all the trappings accompanying them.

The desires of the individual were very rarely fulfilled by British films, or indeed in real life in post-war Britain. Nor were the desires expressed in British films the fairly straightforward ones common to virtually all American films. Achievements in postwar British films tended to be those of the group, not the individual. For example, Ealing comedy films like *Passport to Pimlico* and *Whiskey Galore* have whole groups as collective heroes: the inhabitants of a Scottish isle, or a small borough in London, or a gang of thieves or children. Individuals who do distinguish themselves in Ealing films, like the inventor of the everlasting white suit in *The Man in the White Suit* or the ambitious aristocrat prepared to murder his relatives for the sake of a title in *Kind Hearts and Coronets*, were rarely the unequivocally good heroes in their films. Achievement in British films also tended to be primarily a middle class phenomenon. *Breaking the Sound Barrier*, *Scott of the Antarctic* and *The Dam Busters* are all good examples of these as are are all the substantial number of films about British prisoners of war escaping from German prisoner-of-war camps. There was also, as Raymond Durgnat has noted, a tendency in British films to glorify heroic failure: *Scott of the Antarctic* and *The Magic Box* are both examples of this. [25] Playing the game fairly and losing was more important than winning at any cost.

In addition, there were very few images of successful upward social mobility in British films - but plenty of morality tales like *The Importance of Being Earnest* and *Kind Hearts and Coronets* about what happens to unscrupulous social climbers.

Very much in contrast to these British films, Hollywood has

always, in some senses, been very classless because of unfamiliar locales and accents and a fundamentally egalitarian element in most of its films which the British films simply lacked. Upward social mobility - or the prospect of it - had always been an important part of the American feature film. This message obviously had a powerful appeal to American audiences and also to large sections of the British population. As Gans put it: 'The popularity of American fare is due to some distinctive gratifications which it provides more adequately than the domestic media . . . American films provide themes that appeal to aspirations of the young British working class, whereas the British films and their creators are more concerned with the preoccupations of the middle-aged, middle class audience.' [26]

There was a tendency amongst critics in Britain to be fairly disparaging of popular tastes, to assume that cinemas did little more than to serve as a vent for the baser emotions: 'Most of our British audiences, though they vary from the so-called sophisticated people of the first run London and provincial theaters to the tough audiences of the great midland and northern industrial belt, accept films quite uncritically, only aware vaguely that last week was better than this week, and that next week, judging from the trailer, should be better than either . . . The cinema is for them a place of intense excitement and joy, a vast playground of emotions dammed up by the factory, the office and the repressions of home life.' [27] It was this sort of condescension towards the British mass audience which made it so difficult for many British films to appeal to British audiences.

Notes

1. R. Durgnat, *A Mirror For England*, (Faber, London, 1970, p. 6.
2. Washington Chamber of Commerce, cited in Boothby, Hansard, column 2543, 16 November 1945.
3. J. E. Harley, *Worldwide Influence of the Cinema* (University of Southern California Press, Los Angeles, 1940), and L. A. Handel, *Hollywood Looks At Its Audience* (University of Illinois Press, Urbana, 1950) are both example of this trend. The Motion Picture Association of America's *Juvenile Delinquency. . . A World Problem* (MPEA, New York, 1950), was a direct attempt to undermine any attempts to link adolescent behaviour and films.

4. R. Williams, Jun., 'Changes in Value Orientation in Friedman,
5. W. Wright, *Sixguns and Society, A Structuralist Study Western* (University of California Press, Berkley, 1975).
6. A. Visson, *As Others Sees Us* (Doubleday, Garden City, 1948).
7. 'Film Relations with America', *Documentary News Letter* , no. 6 (1944), p. 1.
8. W. D. Wall and W. A. Simson, 'The Effects of Cinema Attendance on the Behaviour of Adolescents as Seen by Their Contemporaries', *British Journal of Educational Psychology*, vol. 19 (1949), pp. 53-61.
9. Hansard, column 683, 19 November 1946
10. Hansard, Column 2550, 16 November 1945
11. E. Johnston, 'Messengers from a Free Country', *Saturday Review of Literature,* March 4, 1950.
12. W. Wanger, 'Donald Duck and Diplomacy', *Public Opinion Quarterly*, Fall 1950.
13. N. Roddick, *A New Deal in Entertainment; Warner Brothers in the 1930s* (British Film Institute, London, 1983); B. Henderson, 'A Musical Comedy of Empire', *Film Quarterly*, Winter 1981-2.
14. P. Biskind, *Seeing Is Believing: How Hollywood Taught Us to Stop Worrying and Love the Fifties* (Pantheon, New York, 1983); R. Maltby, *Harmless Entertainment; Hollywood and the Ideology of Consensus* (Scarecrow Press, Metuchen, NJ, 1983).
15. Durgnat, *A Mirror for England,* p. 4
16. 'Points Of View', *What's Happening in Hollywood*, no 6, 15 (1948), p. 4.
17. J. P. Mayer, *British Cinemas and Their Audiences* (Dennis Dobson, London, 1948), document # 14.
18. C. Barr, *Ealing Studios* (Cameron and Tayleur, London, 1977).
19. D. Reisman, *et al* . in P. Carter, *Another Part of the Fifties* (Columbia University Press, New York, 1983).
20. J. Feuer, *The Hollywood Musical* (Indiana University Press, Bloomington, 1982).
21. G. Lambert, 'Films and the Idea of Happiness', *Good Living,* (1948), pp. 61-5.
22. Lt.-Col. Derek Walker-Smith, Hansard, column 2559, 16 November 1945.
23. S. Kracauer, 'National Types as Hollywood Sees Them', *Public Opinion Quarterly*, no. 13 (1949).

24. *The Times*, 17 October 1947, p. 5.
25. Durgnat, *Mirror for England*, p. 16.
26. H. J. Gans, *The Social Structure of Popular Culture*, p. 7.
27. R. Manvell, 'Clearing the Air', *Hollywood Quarterly*, vol. 2, no. 2 (1947), p. 176.

Chapter Five

American Stars and British Audiences

> Stars were - they are - what the American film was about,
> what the world went to see American films for, in preference
> to those from all other countries, including their own...the
> film star was the American industry's contribution to film as a
> rapturous art. [1]

> American stars are more popular than American films. [2]

For many cinemagoers, film stars have been as significant and meaningful a part of the film viewing experience as the storylines and themes of the films in which they have appeared. Stars have a complex relationship with the film audience, they are one of the pleasures of the text which the film viewer consumes. In some very simple ways, this is akin to the type of distanced hero worship which historically performers of all sorts and other types of celebrity, such as athletes, and very occasionally politicians, have received from their admirers. However, the film stars' status as mediated characters has made the quality of the adulation which they have received unique and specially potent. Under the conventions of the Hollywood feature film, screen talent is not just part of the film frame like the sets, props and scenery. In some ways, the external physical appearance of screen talent is a part of the *mise-en-scene* of a film, but stars bring much more than a performance or physical appearance to the screen.

For some theorists stars are the primary authors of the films in which they appear. They are in many respects the most significant aspect of those films. For others, like Roland Barthes, stars themselves constitute a text, yielding to a variety of readings and possible interpretations. Interpretations of this sort rarely tend to be concerned with the more broadly sociological and economic considerations which must in the final analysis be part of a discussion of the star system, for screen actors and actresses only become elevated to star status directly in relation to their followings. Unfortunately, most of the serious writing on film stars which does consider the social context within which stars have been created and consumed tends very much towards hagiography, not theory. Richard Dyer's important work on the star phenomenon attempts to synthesize work on the stars, trying to reconcile the sociological and the semiotic approaches.[3]

In the 1940s and 1950s, even writers working for the lightweight, light-hearted film press destined for the cinema audience were conscious of the importance of aspiration as one of the gratifications people received from watching American films. As one wrote:

> Films can alter the way of life of a great many people to a
> certain extent; they can make ordinary working folk more
> actively envious of the higher standard of living that most
> films picture; and they can make people realize the need for
> reforms more quickly than any other medium. [4]

American stars were an important vehicle for these aspirations.

All this emphasis upon 'vitality' in the American feature film is in part an acknowledgment of the significance of the role of screen talent in the American feature film. For most American stars actualized 'life' and 'vitality', and a whole lifestyle, at least as much as the stories in which they appeared, and they did this in a manner quite remote from the style of the British star system. The 'star' phenomenon, the cult of the personality in film, has been an important aspect of American film culture and a valuable merchandising device for the industry ever since Carl Laemmle discovered there was money to be made from giving screen credit to talent and publicizing the attributes and biographies of screen actors and actresses. Laemmle and his peers dicovered that stars, to a much greater extent than specific storylines, could be a source of essentially guaranteed profits for the film producer.

The narrative form of the classical Hollywood film has always been structured around screen performance. One of the basic tenets of the narrative style of the classic realist text manufactured by Hollywood became the representation of a small group of foregrounded characters presented in pyschological depth. This emphasis on screen talent, and the cinematic codes which evolved to render screen talent, such as the use of the close-up, and 'glamour' lighting, made American film significantly different from that which evolved in much of the rest of the world. Although it should be acknowledged that subsequently many other countries, such as India, have adopted star systems based on the American model of spectacle, stardom has always been a characteristic closely tied to the American feature film.

Until the 1950s, when their role as the dominant mass medium was usurped by television, motion pictures were a form of civil religion in the United States in the sense that they have provided an opportunity for the collective celebration of jointly held values. Film viewing was for a time a major social institution, in which large numbers of people collaborated in the consumption of very ritualized culture in stylized surroundings. From this perspective, Hollywood's stars had an important liturgical and symbolic function. They have been the mediators and personification of social values, ideals and ideas. It has been argued, for example, that some stars have represented threatened social values. [5] This is a notion which perhaps sheds light on the different ways in which American and British stars in the postwar decade represented different and possibly competing values.

Leo Lowenthal, for example, noted the changes in the types of individuals who were subject to hero worship during the course of the twentieth century, by making a content analysis of popular biographies written at the time, which he used as a primary indicator of which individuals were most admired at different points in time. Essentially, he noted, that at the turn of the century, society's heroes, were primarily the heroes of production, industrialists and and the other captains of industry, whilst later personalities were heroes of consumption. [6] Richard Dyer warns against making easy connections between this transformation and the development of the United States into a society whose fundamental economic problem was not how to produce enough, but how to dispose of the surpluses which it produced. He argues that the notion that 'the idols expressing in ideological form the economic imperatives of society' is very seductive, but the connections are much less straightforward than this would have us believe. [7] Nevertheless, celebration of conspicuous consumption and the regular display of the material standing of stars in the films and also in the magazine features in which they appeared was an important part of their appeal. There were significant differences in the manner in which these features were stage-managed for British and for American stars. British screen stars were never rooted in the ideology of consumerism in quite the way that American stars were as a matter of course.

Many fan magazines dwelt on the wealth, material possessions and extensive leisure time enjoyed by American stars. They must have been a very heady mixture for the postwar cinemagoer in Britain. All the surveys of British audience reactions conducted at the time include comments like this one: 'I do sit and sigh for the kind of clothes Ginger Rogers and Lana Turner wear and would also be influenced by the Hollywood home with the pretty curtains and marvellous white kitchens if Mr Dalton would let me be.' [8]

Character or Personality?

It is common to talk about films as being the vehicles for this or that star - and quite literally that is how many films have functioned. In the classic Hollywood film, action is supplemented in a very substantial way to screen presence. Often plot has been subordinate to screen presence, serving primarily as a proscenium device to frame the physical appearance and presence of screen talent. Which do we remember more: the actual story of *Casablanca* or Humphrey Bogart's presence/appearance in the film? It is also part of the industrial nature of Hollywood that films and properties are generally selected carefully with specific screen talent in mind for specific roles. Performance on the screen becomes an extension of the 'personality' of the star. It is generally hard to know which is more of a construct: the 'personality' of a star, or the characters he or she populates in specific films.

Stars were important as objects of desire. Audiences responded to not only the physical attributes of a screen actor or actress, but also to what the stars represented, what types and values they represented and what they owned. Film stars have been the focus of a whole complex array of emotions, which are rarely explained by simple sexual attraction. Leo Handel, in one of the first serious and systematic studies of the Hollywood audience, argued that historically audiences tended to express the strongest preference for members of their own sex - implying that the star/audience relationship is not underwritten by straightforward sexual desire. [9] More recently, Garth Jowett, in an excellent attempt to chart the development of film audience and market research, has noted the industry's difficulties in taking advantage of the discovery that in the United States, women like male and female screen performers equally, whilst men, due to their preference for 'action' films, have always had a strong preference for male stars. [10]

There has been some critical work dealing with the relationship between film talent and film text. For example, theories of the star as *auteur* has emerged in the course of discussing the very conspicuous screen presence of Greta Garbo and others. [11] With the exception of the work of Roland Barthes, however, there have been few attempts to delineate the manner in which the film viewer 'reads' the actor or actress in a film, and very little success in quantifying the reactions of the film viewer to the presence on the screen of a favourite star. Barthes' own work is hardly scientific, as illustrated by his attempts to gauge the effects of the 'deified face' of Greta Garbo:

> Garbo still belongs to that moment in cinema when capturing the human face still plunged audiences into the deepest ectasy, when one literally lost oneself in a human image as one would in a philtre, when the face represented a kind of absolute state of the flesh, which could be neither reached nor renounced. [12]

Nor have there been many close studies of specific reading contexts - except for Richard Dyer's recent volume on the reading of specific stars like Judy Garland, or Laura Mulvey's work on the significance of the gaze and scopophilia. [13]

Connery Chappell, the editor of *Picturegoer*, clearly had a strong sense of the rapport between stars and audiences. As he noted in an editorial for British readers:

> The whole glamour and charm of the screen has been carefully built up around the personalities of the players themselves. They are the heroes, the heroines, the rascals and the comics of a shadow world into which millions of us are happy to escape. [14]

The film industry was very aware in a much more pragmatic way of the extent to which star presence was a part of the product they retailed overseas. As Walter Wanger wrote in 1950: 'We (Hollywood) have world-wide acceptance. People everywhere like our subjects; they admire our technique; and they certainly like our stars.' [15]

Few British screen actors or actresses were stars in the American sense: media personalities who maintained a parasocial relationship with their followers. Via an elaborate mechanism of press releases and personal appearances arranged by the studios, rising screen stars and established stars invited the readers of the fan magazines, members of the fan clubs and cinema audiences into their homes and into their pseudo-private lives. The 'star system', which had been created originally as a marketing device, was a significant part of most people's experience of the cinema in the 1940s and 1950s. Not all cinemagoers had the same intense relationship with the stars, but star personalities were invariably foregrounded in popular literature geared towards the cinema audience, in film advertising, and, of course, in the films themselves.

An interesting development after the Second World War was the real emergence of the 'fan' phenomenon in Great Britain. My understanding of this term is extreme involvement between a viewer and a specific screen presence - to be involved with the personality of the star more than narrative action, to have some strong degree of identification with a specific star. Andrew Tudor schematized the depth of intensity characterizing audience-star interactions. He distinguished between high degrees of identification between star and audience, where very strong identification causes the viewer quite literally to project him/herself into the position of a star, and low identification, where audience and star have an emotional affinity, manifested in simple imitation, including the mimicking of physical and behavioural patterns. [16]

Perhaps the most marked evidence of this was the growth of a style of cinema journalism fixed upon the lives of the stars, not film reviews and criticism. There had always been a market in Britain for journals devoted to the lives of the stars, either produced indigenously or imported from the United States. They featured photographs to be used as pin ups by both sexes, story synopses, and a blend of press release and inside gossip. It was a strange mixture which distanced screen talent and yet made them very familiar at the same time. People learnt to desire photographs.

The most prestigious film magazine in Britain, *Picturegoer*, began life in Britain in 1911, but it was only from 1931 onwards that it assumed the form with which we are familiar. In the postwar decade, it had a number of short-lived rivals: *Film Fantasy and Fact* (formerly *Film-Fan Fare*), *Film Post* (1947-1951); *Film Forecast* (1948-1951); *Screen Stories* (1948-1949).

Similarly, there were 'fan' clubs dedicated to developing the followings of individual stars. In the British Film Institute Archives, there are few materials devoted to fandom and the ones that seem most apparent are actually American musical performers. Early tours of Britain by Liberace and Frank Sinatra received a great deal of attention in the lay press for the way in which their fans behaved. The cult of the celebrity was much more widespread and developed in the United States, and this was a clear example of British young people appropriating American behaviour.

At the end of the 1940s, Norah Alexander wrote what appears to be an isolated piece on the fan letter phenomenon, trying to create a profile of the typical fan letter writer by looking at the fan mail received by Richard Attenborough. She noted that fully 80% of his mail was from women, and that all 'invariably betray a strong emotional attachment to the star'. She also noted however, that most of the letters were fixated with sports since 'a surprisingly high proportion of the letters suggest Amazonian qualities strangely at variance with one's usual concept of a film-struck girl'. It took the British industry much longer to learn to exploit these feelings, so that, as Alexander noted, in England 'until quite recently, fan-mail was regarded as a spare-time chore for the general office staff, whilst in American studios 'the fan-mail department is so efficiently organised that the stars complain they seldom see a fan letter'. [17]

The American film industry was much more likely to stage special events where the celebrities could be seen and admired than the British film industry. This was also something that the British film industry learnt to mimic. The first Royal Film Performance took place in November 1946, and was really the first attempt to replicate the form and experience of the Hollywood premiere. It was a chance to mix traditionally British notions of celebrity (the Royal Family), with the new-style elite drawn from the masses emanating from the United States. Interestingly, it was very poorly orchestrated and led to fairly severe public disturbances.

American stars were obliged to invite their followings into their homes via magazine articles, attending public functions, and in many other carefully controlled ways. They also acquired legions of British fans - most of them rather less extreme versions of the fellow whose only ambition in life was to go to Hollywood and marry Deanna

Durbin: 'It is not just calf love or a passing infatuation, but its the real thing.' [18]   Reading J. P. Mayer's assessments of the postwar British audience, and especially the testimony provided by the fans themselves, one gets the impression that most fans were not as extreme in their devotion, and that the most fanatic of fans tended to be drawn from the younger and more impressionable cinemagoers. Richard Dyer says much the same thing: 'particularly intense star-audience relations occur amongst adolescents and women . . .These groups all share a peculiarly intense degree of role/identity conflict and pressure, and an (albeit partial) exclusion from the dominant articulacy of, respectively, adult, male, heterosexual culture.' [19]   At the less extreme end of identification, this type of relationship often assumed the form of straightforward imitation:

> When I saw Gene Tierney wearing a very pretty costume in
> *Laura* I decided to have it copied . . . Films also have an
> influence upon hair styles. When I saw Veronica Lake in *This
> Gun for Hire*, I tried to copy her hair style. However, it did
> not suit me . . . There is a right way and a wrong way of
> holding a cigarette; they do it the right way on the pictures
> and when I begin to smoke I shall do it like Katherine
> Hepburn in *The Philadelphia Story.* [20]

Hollywood had created a very elaborate mechanism for manufacturing stars, who were carefully groomed for stardom. Hollywood stars were remodeled as frequently and quickly as motor car models.

Cinemagoers in Britain in the thirties were encouraged to follow the public lives of native film stars. However, there was really nothing comparable to the big centralized industrial and marketing machinery of Hollywood. One reason for this was that most film publicity in Britain tended to be engineered at the local level. This took the form of 'stunts' created by local and regional film exhibitors and distributors to advertise coming attractions. However, 'stunts' advertising films centred on action, not actors. The star/fan phenomenon only really took a hold on the British cinemagoer after the Second World War. One possible explanation for this was the war itself, when many who were separated from their loved ones had to make do with surrogate relationships with the actors and actresses they saw at the cinema. In this kind of context, charisma became all the more important as part of what it was that audiences purchased at the box office.

Great Expectations: The postwar quality British film was immersed in the past, not the present.

All stills courtesy Theatre Collection, Free Library of Philadelphia

This Happy Breed: British films with a contemporary setting were rare.

Cheaper by the Dozen: An idealized version of the American family in *Cheaper by the Dozen.*

It's A Date: American stars like Deanna Durbin, had a tremendous following in Great Britain.

How Green Was My Valley: American films rarely dealt with British society in a serious contemporary setting. *How Green Was My Valley* was a typical romanticizing of British family life.

Laura: The attire of the actors and actresses exerted a powerful influence over the British filmgoer. Gene Tierney's costumes in *Laura* were the envy of many British women with few ration coupons.

Father of the Bride: American middle class family life was depicted in a very luxurious manner in the films of the fifties.

How To Marry A Millionaire: American films of the fifties celebrated conspicuous consumption.

After the war, fan clubs and fan magazines proliferated. There would almost certainly have many more magazines but for the postwar paper shortage. There was a rapid turnover of magazines of this type, and they acquired a fairly large cumulative circulation. Most of these periodicals carried little except gossip about film stars, usually accompanied by photographs of the stars suitable for pin-up purposes. The pin-up for both sexes and featuring both sexes also had really come into its own during the Second World War. Again, as Mary Beth Haralovitch has argued recently, this was largely engineered by the film industry itself. [21]

True Brits

Surprisingly, it was fairly common for the most prominently featured stars in British film magazines to be British. The J. Arthur Rank Organization had begun to develop certain individuals as screen 'personalities', recognizing that the presence of 'stars' in specific films made all the difference at the box office. As the only concern ever to equal the size of one of the Hollywood studios, Rank was essentially the first British studio in a position to push and really exploit the star system. The star system was only useful to a studio able to maintain a sustained and coherent body of film production. Rank began to capitalize on stars such as James Mason and Stewart Granger, who were essentially matinee idols very much along American lines, and who were the first British male leads to ever list above American leading men in polls of audience preferences. The Bernstein Questionnaire placed Mason and Stewart in first and second place in the poll, Mason receiving 27% of the votes cast and Granger 8% . [22]

One interesting aspect of the star system is its ability to reconcile the exceptional and the typical. The myth of stardom maintained that stars were ordinary people who had worked very hard and had achieved extraordinary success and good fortune. Ostensibly, anybody could be a star. As one of Mayer's contributors noted: 'I have read in film books that it was going to the films such a lot that made Van Johnson positive that he wanted to be an actor.' [23] One took the first step towards being a star oneself, then, by going to the cinema. However, the way in which the British film star was 'typical' or 'ordinary' was quite different from the manner in which the American star exemplifed these traits.

Britain's most successful screen performers in the 1930s, George Formby and Gracie Fields, had both made a cult of being ordinary and down-to-earth. This was in no way similar to the demigod status enjoyed by their peers in Hollywood. It is inconceivable to imagine the homely Formby or the girl-next-door Fields at the heart of anybody's fantasies. The war changed a lot of this: people wanted more romance in their otherwise rather drab lives, whereas Formby and Fields' main appeal had been that they were just like the provincial audiences who went to their films, experiencing the same things and living in the same towns. The cognitive deprivation experienced by virtually all British people during the war continued well into the following decade. Most had a narrow range of experiences: little travel, few holidays, a life of extreme regimentation and utility furniture. This was a fertile ground for the birth of a star system along Hollywood lines.

Nice people doing nice things

Postwar Britain had a markedly different pantheon of native talent, including stars who had many more of the attributes of their American counterparts than their predecessors. Its principal members changed during the course of the decade, and it would be wrong to suggest that they were a homogeneous group. The appeal of James Mason and Stewart Granger at the end of the war is perhaps not hard to understand, and Dirk Bogarde soon afterwards made the same kind of appeal to the women in the cinema audience. Anna Neagle and Michael Wilding were also members of this group starting in the late forties. Neagle and Wilding appeared in a series of films produced by Herbert Wilcox, Neagle's husband, which have much of the feel of the Astaire-Rogers films a decade earlier. Light musical comedies in upper class settings, like *The Courtneys of Curzon Street* and *Maytime in Mayfair* were basically the 'white telephone' films of their era, and exercised a powerful appeal to escapists. As Wilson D'Arne said in defence of the Neagle films: 'The highbrows could look down their noses if they wished, but you will find no gloom in the Neagle films. They are almost always simple tales, simply told, dealing in the main with nice people doing nice things.' [24]

Generally, it was the men who dominated the lists of people's star preferences - a bias which is still true today in fact, as demonstrated by the way in which male stars have almost invariably proved more 'bankable' than female stars. In the late forties and early fifties, a stable of British leading men emerged who, unlike Mason and Granger, did not imply they would be leaving for Hollywood at the first possible opportunity. Richard Todd and Anthony Steel, both always described as 'typically British' in the British fan magazines, were examples of British leading men who seemed to be the sort of screen representation of the British hero whom audiences were seeking. Attempting to generalize as to the qualities these leading men stood for, Raymond Durgnat described John Mills, Richard Attenborough, John Gregson, Dirk Bogarde and Donald Sinden as: 'grown up boys, trusting, vulnerable, decently worried'. [25]

Perhaps the quintessential example of a British star who was 'manufactured' by the system was Dirk Bogarde . His insider's view of the star-making process reveals the way in which the Rank Organization carefully fed the fan press material about the stars and manipulated personal appearances to develop public interest in certain stars. [26] If the American experience is anything to go by, fan magazines were very unquestioning in their acceptance and reproduction of studio press releases, and studio publicity and press release copy invariably found its way into the columns of the fan magazines and the lay press. [27]

Rank also created a mechanism for finding stars. Its Company of Youth scheme was supposedly a means of locating and grooming young talent for the screen. In the late forties, Rank received over 300 letters a week asking about being admitted to the programme. Few stars ever graduated from the Company, which was probably most important as a source of fantasy aspirations for fans who themselves dreamed of going into the movies. The Company of Youth scheme reinforced the notion that watching films was only slightly removed from appearing in them. [28]

In the postwar decade the American studios began to dismantle the star system, at just about the same time that Rank was developing one in Great Britain. In Hollywood, extensive lists of contract players became a liability, not an asset, when the studios began to face severe financial problems, so they began to cut back on their stables of potential stars as an economy measure. It was still possible for an 'unknown' to become a star in postwar Hollywood. In 1946, for example, Burt Lancaster was offered seven Hollywood contracts on the basis of a three week appearance in a Broadway show. In fact, Hollywood was deluged by returning servicemen trying to get into the film industry. But, in general, the notion of grooming and manufacturing stars became much less common.

Critics have often noted a qualitative difference between the stars of the late 1940s and early 1950s and those who had worked in Hollywood's 'golden age'. There was something very synthetic about Doris Day, Debbie Reynolds and Rock Hudson. Also, as an anonymous publicity man told Hollis Alpert: 'The stars are losing their glamour. Its next to impossible to get Burt Lancaster into columns these days. He's too serious. The public prefers its stars to behave a little crazy. Look what that dope party did for Bob Mitchum! Look how Deborah Kerr's divorce troubles sent her price way up! Who wants to form a fan club for a businessman!' [29]

Many American stars maintained large followings in Great Britain. Denied the prospect of Hollywood premieres and personal appearances, fans had to make do with going to the cinema, voraciously consuming magazines, and joining fan clubs. If all this seems extreme and adolescent, it is perhaps a reflection of the changing demographics of the British cinema audience in the 1940s and 1950s. Gans and the other researchers discovered that British audiences expressed stronger preferences for American stars than they did for specific American films. In addition, they also discovered that expressed preferences were much stronger in the case of leading men than in the case of leading women:

> Although British audiences were reputed to like glamour, they
> generally seem to prefer male stars to female ones. The popular
> American actresses are stars like Doris Day, who represent
> beauty, but in an unthreatening and simple sentimental form;
> or those who portray Hollywood glamour queens from a
> humorous perspective. [30]

Would it be fair to argue that the British star system was less fixated upon physical appearances than Hollywood and that therefore stars did not become in such a straightforward way the objects of desire? Few British stars relied upon their physique and physiognomy in the way that Hollywood talent did, although significantly those British stars who ultimately migrated to Hollywood came closest to resembling their Hollywood peers. 'Glamour', then, did not play the same role in star and audience relationships that it did in the United States. With few exceptions, John Mills and his contemporaries were admired more for the values they represented rather than for their external physical appearance. In an era when the British film industry was fighting for the 'British film', it was important that the studios could field a 'British film star'. Initially, their model was that of the glamorous Hollywood star. Hence, when James Mason wrote an article chastising British films for their lack of 'glamour' he set off a minor crisis within the industry. [31] Later, emerging British stars seemed to personify more characteristically British traits and were not such straightforward carbon copies of American-style stars.

Despite Rank's efforts in the area of developing its own stable of talent, and the real emergence of a group of actors who were box office material in British films, it seems to be the case that American stars remained popular with British audiences throughout the postwar decade, and it was partly on their account that American films continued to dominate British screens.

Notes

1. J. Kobal, *Film Star Portraits of the Fifties*, (Peter Smith, Magnolia, MA., 1980), p. v.
2. H. Gans, 'American Films and TV Programs on British Screens' unpublished PhD dissertation, University of Pennsylvania, 1959, p. 30.
3. R. Dyer, *The Stars* (British Film Institute, London, 1979).
4. Malcolm Ruy Wade, 'Cinema of the Future', *Film Fantasy and Fact*, vol. 1, no. 2, pp. 12, 15.
5. See, for example, C. Eckhert, 'Shirley Temple and the House of Rockefeller', *Jump Cut*, no. 2 (July-August 1974), pp. 1, 17-20.
6. L Lowenthal, *Literature, Popular Culture and Mass Society*, (Prentice-Hall, Englewood Cliffs, 1961), p. 115.
7. Dyer, *Stars*, p. 45.
8. J. P.Mayer, *British Cinemas and Their Audiences* (Dennis Dobson, London, 1948), document # 8.
9. L. Handel, *Hollywood Looks At Its Audience* (University of

Illinois Press, Urbana, 1950).

10. G. S. Jowett, 'Giving Them What They Want: Movie Audience Research Before 1950', in B. Austin (ed.), *Current Research in Film Volume 1: Audiences, Economics and Law* (Ablex, New Jersey, 1985).

11. B. Erkkila, 'Greta Garbo: Sailing Beyond the Frame', *Critical Inquiry*, no. 11, 1985, pp. 595-619

12. R. Barthes, 'The Face of Garbo', *Mythologies* (Granada, London, 1973), p. 56.

13. L. Mulvey, 'Visual Pleasure and Narrative Cinema', *Screen*, vol. 16 (1975), pp. 6-18.

14. *Picturegoer Film Annual*, 1949.

15. W. Wanger, 'Donald Duck and Diplomacy', *Public Opinion Quarterly*, vol 14, no. 2 (1950), pp. 443-52.

16. A. Tudor, *Image and Influence: Studies in the Sociology of Film* (St Martin's Press, New York, 1975).

17. N. Alexander, 'Frustrated, Lonely and Peculiar', in J. Sutro (ed.), *Diversion* (Max Parrish, London, 1950), pp. 70-7.

18. J. P. Mayer, *Sociology of the Film* (Faber, London, 1946), document # 1.

19. Dyer, *Stars*.

20. Mayer, *Sociology of Film*, document # 27, p. 215.

21. M. B. Haralovitch, 'Film Advertising, the Film Industry and the Pin-up: The Industry's Accommodations to Social Forces in the 1940s', in Austin, *Current Research in Film*.

22. Bernstein Questionnaire p. 2a.

23. Mayer, *Sociology of Film*, document # 3, pp. 184-5.

24. 'The Favourites: Anna Neagle', *Picturegoer Annual*, 1949, pp.6-7.

25. R. Durgnat, *A Mirror for England* (Faber, London, 1970), p. 142.

26. D. Bogarde, *Snakes and Ladders* (Chatto and Windus, London, 1978), p. 135.

27. *'Hollywood's Barkers'*, unidentifed clipping, British Film Institute.

28. 'Stars and Films of Tomorrow', *Film Post*, Autumn, 1947

29. H. Alpert, *The Dreams and the Dreamers*, cited in Dyer, *Stars* p. 39.

30. Gans,'American Films', p. 30.

31. J. Mason, *Before I Forget*, (Hamish Hamilton, London, 1981), p. 157.

Chapter Six

The Hollywood Embargo:
Hollywood versus the British Government

> The foreign film market for American films is probably more important to the motion picture industry as a fraction of total business done than is the foreign market for any other finished product industries. [1]

> We are importing about four fifths of our screen entertainment at an annual cost of the dollar equivalent of about £18,000,000, while our receipts from the showing of our films in America - a market four times the size of ours - amount to barely one tenth, or even one twentieth of this amount. [2]

The international market has always been very important to Hollywood. This was never truer than in the decade after the Second World War, when the decline of the domestic film market and major changes in the structure of the film industry made the overseas market vital. In 1945, total cinema admissions in the United States totalled 1,450 million, going down to 1,376 million in 1950 and 1,326 million by 1955. These figures become much more revealing when viewed as a percentage of the proportion of individuals' personal income devoted to recreation. In 1945, a massive 23.6% of personal income was spent at the cinema, down to 12.3% by 1950 and 9.4% by 1955. [3] Furthermore, at precisely the same time that the film industry was having to compete with other forms of recreation for consumers' dollars, and commercial television - which was free, the Paramount Decrees (1948) effectively divorced film producers from film exhibition in the United States, thereby ending the arrangements between producers and exhibitors which had essentially guaranteed the profits of the film industry.

In 1955, the U.S. Department of Commerce estimated that American films accounted for 68% of playing time in the world's cinemas. This was a slight decrease from 1951, when the figure was 74%. The number of cinemas increased during this period, from 99,543 worldwide in 1951 to 108,537 in 1955. 63,057 of these cinemas were in Europe, which constituted the biggest single market for American films, and throughout the period Britain was the biggest single customer in this market. [4]

During the war, American film producers and distributors had willingly accepted government restrictions and strict regulation over the activities in Britain. This had included limiting the number of American films shown on British screens, and also the amount of sterling taken out of Britain. The mechanisms were therefore in place to maintain these procedures during peacetime, although American film prodcuers felt that they were entitled to full and unrestricted control over their markets in Britain because of the extent to which they had co-operated with the government during the war. The war also had a number of beneficial consequences for the British film industry, and perhaps of special significance was the development of the market for British films in the United States during the war. Sidney Bernstein left the chairmanship of Granada cinemas to build the market for British films in the United States. He established a rota system, whereby each of the major American producers agreed to take a British feature film and two short films each year for the duration of the war, and to distribute these on an equal footing with their own films in the United States.

British producers had other reasons for optimism after the war. The sixth Bernstein questionnaire, conducted in late 1946, indicated that cinema audiences in Britain had developed a taste for British films and stars, as discussed in an earlier chapter. For the first time, serious British actors and matinee idols like James Mason and Stewart Granger ranked above American stars in British audience preferences. There was a marked preference for British films too. At the same time, these same stars had begun to develop followings in the United States, and it became an issue of national importance to try and keep Britain's highest paid stars from leaving for the lures of Hollywood. A number of the most prestigious British films had performed well in the United States market and the Rank Organization was arranging through its connections with Universal Pictures for the mass ditribution of British features in the United States, and with Eagle-Lion for distribution throughout the rest of the world.

In hindsight, only the most narrowly optimistic and ill-informed members of the film industry could have believed that the wartime prosperity of the British film industry was likely to continue into the peace. The war closed down over 50% of Britain's film production capacity. Many studios had been turned over to other uses, such as storage and aircraft production, whilst others had been requisitioned for the production of government films. [5] During the war, filmmakers had learnt to make maximum use of the surviving sound stages, and had developed a location aesthetic which placed minimal demands upon sound stages. Wartime hits like *In Which We Serve*, *Waterloo Road* and *Target for Tonight* had made a virtue out of their modest production values, and had placed fairly light demands on existing studio space. At the time, it was generally acknowledged that the synthesis of actuality and fictional approaches which occurred in wartime British directors created a form which was uniquely suited to telling the story of Britain at war. As Roger Manvell put it at the time:

> These men all brought to the British screen a new vitality and individuality which was a direct product of the war years. They were consciously reacting against the streamlined showmanship of Hollywood. The work of these directors was greatly influenced by pre-war and wartime documentary. It was bound to the national life of Britain, to our people, our cities and our rich and varied countryside. [6]

The government also found that exhibitors during the war were more willing than they had been to present British films, and in any event they had screentime to spare because of the restrictions on American imports.

The war brought prosperity to Britain's film duopoly, the J. Arthur Rank Organization and the Associated British Picture Corporation. Rank grew tremendously in all parts of the industry during the war, whilst ABPC had all its studio space requisitioned and ceased film production for the duration of the war. The British government's intention was to keep the two strong, particularly the Rank Organization, so that it could 'remain effective for meeting and possibly dealing with American competition'. [7] The situation was very complicated, because the two companies intended to 'deal with' the American film industry were very largely owned by United States companies. Twentieth Century Fox had major holdings in Gaumont British, United Artists had a large block of shares in Odeon, and Warner Brothers had virtual control of ABC. [8] In addition, Britain's independent producers were perennially in trouble. They lacked the guaranteed markets of the big producers and it was largely for their benefit that the government initiated a Film Production Council in late 1947.

It is hard to reconcile Britain's importance as an overseas market for Hollywood in the years after the war with its diminutive status as a market for feature films today. [9] After 1945, peace brought instability to Hollywood, which was plagued increasingly by the threat of divestiture and increasing labour unrest amongst studio workers. By 1947, earnings from the British market often made the difference between profit and loss for the American film industry. In 1946, Hollywood's 'Big Eight' recorded aggregate earnings of $172,000,000 a year; $70,000,000 of this was claimed as taxes and $36,000,000 was paid out in dividends. During the same period, earnings from the British market totalled $68,000,000, or nearly double total company dividends for that year. [10]

In the thirties, American studios were obligated to invest in British production under the provisions of the quota regulations. Successive cinematograph films acts tried to restrict American imports and encourage British feature film production. This led to a vast number of low budget 'quota' films intended to obey the letter but not the spirit of the quota laws. British exhibitors therefore had a source of nominally 'British' films which they could show to fulfil their legal commitment to show British films. The large number of quota films produced in the 1930s was largely responsible for overstating the state of health of the British film production end of the industry, so that according to many estimates, such as that of Legg and Klingender, the total number of British films ranked only second to Hollywood in terms of annual output. [11] The quota situation was greatly improved during the war, when 'quota quickie' production essentially ceased.

After the war, despite the advantages which had accrued to British producers, feature film production in Great Britain remained at extremely modest levels. In 1945, Britain produced only 24 first feature films, and even two years later the British film industry produced only 49 films. [12] It was always very difficult for exhibitors to fulfil their quota obligations for British films. In 1946, the quota stood at 15%, which was a proportion of an exhibitor's total screentime, not necessarily 15% of the feature films he showed, which had to be made in Britain. In the same year, 972 exhibitors were reported for defaulting on their quota commitments. In other words, nearly one fifth of Britain's exhibitors showed fewer British films than they were legally obliged to show in their theatres. The following year, when the quota had been raised to 17.5% there were 1,328 defaults. [13] There were simply not enough British feature films being produced to meet even the minimum quota demands for exhibiting British feature films laid down by the government. Finally, after 20 years, the government began to appreciate that it was extremely hard to control both the business practices and audience preferences by legislation alone.

At the governmental level, film policy was generally discussed in conjunction with wider economic policy. Anglo-American economic relations after the war seemed in some way to be replicated perfectly in microcosm in negotiations over the market in films between Britain and the United States. In the immediate postwar years, more than 40% of the total value of American exports to Great Britain consisted of just two commodities, tobacco and films. Their combined value was initially greater than the total value of British exports to the United States. Government statements about planning economic recovery and improving the balance of trade invariably turned to the issue of spending precious dollars on luxuries like tobacco and films. Hugh Dalton, whilst Chancellor of the Exchequer, was prone to talk in very simple terms of 'food before fags' and 'food before films'. [14] These were clearly understood slogans that one suspects did little to make heavier taxes on cigarettes or more British films in the cinema any more palatable to the general public. The Labour government was adamant that American revenues from the British market had to be strictly limited, whilst Hollywood was equally convinced that it was entitled to cultivate the British film market. In most other economic spheres too, the Americans valued Britain more as a market for their goods, than as a supplier of raw materials and finished manufactures. The United States was anxious to keep Britain away from any protectionist measures, and yet the American government wanted to do nothing which might undermine the security and economic wellbeing of her closest ally. As the British position was stated in a meeting between government and industry representatives in August 1947:

'It is both politically and financially impossible for us to allow 70,000,000 dollars worth of food to go out of the United Kingdom'. However, at this same meeting, Eric Johnston, head of the Motion Picture Association of America was so intransigent in protecting American earnings in the United Kingdom, that British officials concluded that the MPAA concessions 'came down to one point - that they (Hollywood) needed earnings from our market and that it was quite likely that our people needed their films.' [15]

The extent to which people were willing to forego other items to enable the country to pay for its food bill was constantly under discussion in the 1940s. In February 1947, precisely the time when the country was running on short time everywhere and Britain's economic prospects were especially grim, the Gallup Organization asked people what they would like to see purchased with the American loan. 40% of those asked wanted the loan to be spent on machinery, 11% suggested tobacco, and only 4% advocated spending the money on films. Significantly, fully 30% of those asked were opposed to the loan. It is hard to know the value of responses like this where the questions and the range of possible answers were framed by the pollsters themselves. Nevertheless, this series of responses implies that although people may have valued their visits to the cinema, and may have been influenced by what they saw there, they placed a higher priority on industrial recovery. [16]

The issue of what ought to be sacrificed in order to purchase American films was aired regularly in the House of Commons. As Robert Boothby confessed there, 'I have a great admiration for the acting of Mr Humphrey Bogart . . . Nevertheless, as I am compelled to choose between Bogart and bacon, I am bound to choose bacon at the present time.' [17] The British film industry's yearbook was equally succinct: 'Until the general economic recovery of the country has been completed, only the irreducible minimum of dollars can be spent on films when food and machine tools must obviously have priority.' [18]

The governments of many other countries had come to the same conclusions about limiting their citizens' consumption of American films. Events in France, Denmark, Australia and elsewhere paralleled events in Britain quite closely. In Denmark, for example, the government forbade exhibitors from showing American films at any one theatre for more than 28 weeks in any one year.

The growing hostility of foreign governments to the incursions of

American films compelled the Motion Picture Association of America to devote a much greater amount of energy to cultivating the overseas markets than it had before the war. A new body, the Motion Picture Export Association, was established in 1946, with the quite specific brief of working to promote the American feature film overseas. It also established a foreign information bureau, which supplied film producers with information about foreign countries they intended depicting in their films. Throughout negotiations with foreign governments, the MPAA and the MPEA were headed by Eric Johnston, a self-made businessman with aspirations to the Republican presidential nomination, and a very able negotiator.

In Britain, a number of schemes to limit the number of American films imported into Great Britain were considered. These included plans to encourage American film production for the British market within Britain; proposals to freeze part or all of American earnings in Britain; and plans to permit the studios to take revenues out of Britain equivalent to the earnings of British films in the United States. [19]

The British government had been astonished when the generous terms of the Lease-Lend scheme were terminated within days after the defeat of Japan. This had actually been one of the provisions of the original agreement, but not one which the British government had assumed would be implemented immediately. Britain thought the immediate cancellation of Lease-Lend very sharp practice. Eventually, another loan was negotiated, but the terms were very harsh and effectively sabotaged the propects for a speedy economic recovery in Britain. As Boothby noted:

> If the government have decided to borrow a very large sum at a considerable rate of interest from the United States and to go back to the gold standard and multilateral trade without discrimination as the price, then I suppose the film industry will have to be included in the general 'sell out' of Great Britain. In this case, however, I think we should be well advised to make an immediate application for entry, as a 49th state, into the United States of America; and move ourselves over to Washington in order to get some of the advantages, instead of only the disadvantages, of complete economic control by the United States. [20]

The new loan agreement's terms included a return to dollar-sterling convertibility within a year after the loan being made. This had especially adverse consequences for the British economy. With the exception of the United States itself, the whole of the postwar world was locked in a dollar famine. One immediate result of these loan terms was that all those countries with holdings in sterling began converting them into dollars, so that ultimately Britain's American loan went largely towards paying for this conversion of dollars to pounds whilst trying to shore up the pound on the international money market.

In March 1947, Prime Minister Attlee introduced a three day debate on economic affairs in the House of Commons. The clash between the Labour government's brand of socialism and the United States' commitment to free enterprise came to the foreground of this debate. The American film industry was in many ways the epitome of American free enterprise and felt obliged to recapitulate its ideology in its films. As Nathan Golden, the head of Motion Picture Division at the Department of Commerce, put it:

> U.S. films have always presented the American way of life and have exemplified the workings of a real democratic nation but today our films are at variance with powerful adverse ideologies. Totalitarian or near-totalitarian influence has spread to such a point that in many countries falling within its orbit nationalisation of industry is being enforced and trade in commodities is under complete government control. [21]

The large sums spent on tobacco and films figured prominently in Attlee's speech. There was no intention at this point, however, of formally limiting sterling expenditure on either of these luxuries, which many Labour Members of Parliament considered were basic necessities. This view was not shared by the Conservatives, which is perhaps a little surprising, given their traditionally strong ties with the film industry. As Lord Beveridge noted in a House of Lords debate on 22 April 1947:

> Was there any real reason why the number of dollars spent on unessentials like tobacco and films should be left to be determined by the consumer while dollars spent for much more essential purposes were rigidly limited by the Government? [22]

Britain's economic crisis mounted during the spring and summer of 1947. The American loan ran out very quickly, and the eventual devaluation of the British pound seemed inevitable. Finally, on August 6 1947, in an unusually impassioned speech, Prime Minister Attlee proclaimed that a 'Second Battle of Britain' was taking place - this time on the economic front. Once again, tobacco and film revenues were placed on the frontline of the discussion of Anglo-American economic relations and the state of the national economy. As part of a very wide-ranging series of measures intended to support the ailing pound, Attlee announced that no more than 25% of the receipts from the rental of American films would be allowed out of Britain. The balance of American film rental receipts was to be appropriated by the government. Although this move was widely criticized as rash and insufficiently premeditated, in fact the British government had been planning this move for at least three months. In May 1947, the Board of Trade had written to the head of the British delegation at the meeting of the International Trade Organization in Geneva, informing him that the imposition of this tax was imminent, and he should negotiate with this in mind. [23] This was important news for the British delegation, since the whole rationale for the Geneva meetings was actually the removal of barriers to international trade.

Attlee announced that Britain's total import bill between mid-1947 and mid-1948 would hopefully amount to some £1,700,000,000. It is useful for purposes of comparison and perspective to note that American box office revenues from Great Britain in the previous year had totalled only £17,000,000. Historically, the British government had always taxed box office returns in some form or other. Furthermore, during the war, entertainments tax, levied on each cinema seat, had yielded a very substantial income to the exchequer. However, the government had never taxed producers' and distributors' gross receipts before, and the film trade in Britain and the United States alike were shocked and unprepared for draconian measures which threatened to confiscate fully three-quarters of their earnings. J. Arthur Rank, for example, normally very close to the government in film matters, was caught unawares and had a series of negotiations with American distributors ruined by the new *ad valorem* tax. [24] In the United States, the film industry's reaction was both prompt and predictable. Fifty representatives of the Motion Picture Association of America met together for over three hours in New York City on August 8th.

They decided to cease exporting films to Britain completely until the British tax on their receipts was lifted. This was precisely the same response they had given to tariff barriers erected by governments in Scandinavia, Australia and elsewhere. The head of the Motion Picture Association of America, Eric Johnston, noted: 'If the British do not want American pictures, that is one thing, if they do, they should not expect to get a dollar's worth of film for 25 cents.' [25] Since American distributors and producers had previously received perhaps a quarter of the total revenues their films generated in Britain, after entertainments tax, the exhibitor's share and costs, and their own costs in Britain, as Cheever Cowdin, the chairman of Universal Pictures commented, the new tax permitted American companies to receive less than 4% of the total paid in at the British box office. [26]

The American industry's position was clear: the new *ad valorem* tax was regarded as essentially punitive and confiscatory. Hollywood was surprised that the American government was not more openly hostile to the actions of their British ally. As an editorial in *Variety* proclaimed:

> It is an economic, not an ideological battle. Our American
> government should tackle this problem ... The very industry
> which, for so many years has brought much-needed business
> and a dream of better things to come into the hearts of millions
> of men and women abroad, now is being kicked around like a
> football. [27]

Reading beyond the press releases in the lay and trade newspapers, as far as Hollywood and American business in general were concerned, the dispute with Britain was an ideological as much as an economic struggle. Hollywood, whose chief spokesperson, Eric Johnston, was the former three times president of the United States Chamber of Commerce, was passionately committed to the free enterprise system, and so found much of what was happening as part of the 'socialist experiment' in Britain unacceptable. As Eric Johnston wrote in his treatise on 'partnership capitalism', as he termed it in his best-selling book, *We're All In It*:

> Many Americans are skeptical of Western Europe's social-
> economic experiments. We don't question Europe's right to turn
> to socialism but we have a big question mark as to whether
> socialism can create abundance and at the same time maintain a

free society . . . (European socialists). . . are wondering if they have moved too fast with nationalisation of industries. . . And they are finding out the hard way that ideology is no substitute for human nature; that the incentive motive is deeply ingrained in all men, and that man simply has to have an incentive to produce, or he won't. [28]

Hollywood, furthermore, had many supporters from the increasingly conservative American political establishment.

The British government was aware that, although the film industry was an extremely powerful lobby in the United States, the American government was more concerned about stabilizing the British economy, rather than with Hollywood's short-term economic interests. The head of the Motion Picture Division of the Department of Commerce spoke for the American government as a whole when he noted that American film receipts jeopardized Europe's economic recovery, for, as he noted, 'There is not a country in Europe, with the exception of Belgium and Switzerland, that has sufficient dollars available to pay for American films.' [29] As Munro at the British embassy in Washington noted for the British Foreign Office in a top secret telegram in late August 1947, the American Department of State thought the British tax scheme was 'going over very satisfactorily', except for the pressure being exerted by Hollywood, which he thought was 'probably the most powerful propaganda and public relations machine in the world.' [30]

There was a great deal of fairly overt support for the British position within the American government. When Johnston went directly to President Truman, he made a strong case for tying the Anglo-American film trade directly to American financial aid for Britain. A memorandum on a meeting between Johnston and the British ambassador in Washington noted that although Johnston denied 'any attempt to influence with threats about E.R.P. (European Recovery Program) or our position of priority in E.R.P.', he admitted at the same meeting that he had 'told the whole story to President Truman', who thought that 'the U.S.A. and the United Kingdom might as well throw their whole Havana Charter into the waste paper basket'.[31]

The immediate reaction of the British film trade to the new tax and the American embargo was divided. Most British producers promised that they would fill the gap created by the embargo, since they had perhaps six months before the supply of American films already in the country had become depleted. J. Arthur Rank announced that his companies would produce 48 new films within a year. British exhibitors, however, predicted that cinemas would begin to close down at the beginning of 1948, when they felt that the shortfall of American films would take effect. As W.R. Fuller, General Secretary of the Cinematograph Exhibitors Association noted only days after the embargo had been instituted, 'If the American withdrawal continues, it is only a matter of time before all British kinemas close.' [32] Exhibitors were also very dubious about the ability of British producers to fulfil the demands of British cinema audiences, who in any event they felt would not be easily weaned over to British films.

The American embargo was optimistically viewed by some as the opportunity for British producers to compete with their American rivals on terms which, for once, were favourable to them. In Britain, producers had already devised new working methods intended to reduce the demand for studio space, since lack of studio space was often held to blame for hindering British film production. A good example of this was the 'independent frame' technique developed by David Rawnsley and a group of specialists assembled at the Film Research Department of Production Facilities Ltd. The 'independent frame' was widely touted in the film industry's journals at the time as a means of minimizing demands on sound stages. It essentially entailed maximizing pre-production, and also the use of laboratory process work, including front and rear projection, so as to limit set changes and work on location. This technique, which in many ways resembled Hitchcock's experiments in films like *Rope* and *Stage Fright*, the latter a film he made in Britain at this time, was intended to produce films in a very streamlined and cost-effective fashion which actually anticipated many of the production techniques of studio television. [33]

The American film industry, naturally enough, disparaged the British producers' attempts to fill the gap created by the shortfall in available films. They characterized the British effort as a 'flop'. [34] From their side of the Atlantic, they could see very little actual production in Britain. In addition, the major American studios added to the lack of activity by deliberately curtailing film production at their own film production facilities in England.

The British government took a very firm stand on the films issue. Defeat on this point might have been relatively insubstantial in terms of the overall savings to the national balance of payments, but it would be very symptomatic of shortcomings in Britain's overall postwar economic policies. The Labour government was therefore at great pains to reduce American film imports, and a primary way of doing this was to encourage the growth of the indigenous film industry.

Opinions about the feelings of the general public on the subject of the American embargo varied. Within the film trade, it was generally felt that there was a very pronounced preference for American feature films which would not be denied. There were many critics like C. A. Lejeune, however, who thought that 'the average Englishman is too deeply concerned with essential shortages, too busy worrying about food and fuel and clothes and petrol rationing to care overmuch where his pictures come from, or indeed, whether they come at all.' [35] Her comments are supported by a Gallup Poll taken at the time. When asked, 'If the tax on U.S.A. films means that we get no more American films after a few months, should the tax remain, or be removed?' fully 58% of those asked said the tax should be kept, and only 28% said it ought to be removed. [36]

In practical terms, the backlog of American feature films already in Britain awaiting first time release and the possibility of re-releasing popular feature films were sufficient to span a considerable amount of time until agreement between the British government and the American film industry was reached. Significantly, neither of these sets of films were subject to the new tax. Negotiations between state and industry continued throughout the winter and early spring of 1948.

The MPAA offered many alternatives to the *ad valorem* tax. The favourite proposal was to freeze a percentage of American earnings in Britain and to re-invest them there. The major drawback to this scheme, from the British point of view, was that in the long run it promised to extend American economic control in Britain and to make American film rentals even more lucrative, albeit that revenues might be temporarily deferred. This also raised the issue of what kind of investments could be made with American pound earnings kept in Britain. If they were invested in the British film industry, then British producers would become even more financially dependent on American funds. If invested in other areas - for example, it was suggested that American capital ought to be invested in British hotels and other service industries - then American control would be extended into other domains.

Great Expectations

The United States has always been something of a mirage for British film producers. It constitutes the biggest single market for films in the world and the only major market accessible to the British with a common language. Historically, America has always beckoned, as a market and also as a lure for British talent. It was success in the American market which was the initial basis for the success and reputation of Alexander Korda, since he was practically the first British producer - via Hungary and Hollywood - to sell a film in the international market which also did good business in North America. Ever since film has been an industry, the United States has had half the world's cinema seats and generated well in excess of 50% of the total global cinema box office each year. For British producers, success in the American market was in many ways as crucial as success in competing with Hollywood in the domestic market in Britain.

During the Second World War, the Rank Organization decided that spectacle was the key to the American market, just as it had been for Korda and a small number of British films in the 1930s. Rank therefore funded the production of a small number of 'quality' films made with American distribution in mind. Gabriel Pascal's *Caesar and Cleopatra*, a notoriously extravagant production which did much to discredit the British film industry through tales in the popular press about transporting sand to Egypt and other excesses, was the archetypical 'quality' British film. It failed as an attempt to outdo the spectacle which was a staple of many American feature films. [37] It actually did very poorly in the United States, where it was seen by the film trade and by the mass audience as a tired imitation of a Cecil B. De Mille biblical epic. Rank's salesmen in the United States put on a magnificent sales campaign, and the film was given a major first run release. However, it did very poorly at the box office, when word of mouth began to work against the film, and it ended up doing very little business. Rank had spent some $175,000 on 350 Technicolor prints, and returns from the United States did not even cover the costs of making these prints. [38]

94

British film marketing strategies in the United States never overcame the American studios' control of distribution and exhibition in their own country. However, divestiture and the dismemberment of the studio system soon after the war promised to give British films new opportunities in the United States. Since the 1920s, the practices of block and blind booking had essentially guaranteed the profits of the major studios. The studios controlled first-run cinemas in the major markets directly through ownership, and independent cinemas through their control of the product. Exhibitors were obliged to buy films in groups, not individually, and often sight unseen. In 1938, the American government had begun to act against this oligopoly control by moving first against Paramount, hoping to ultimately establish a precedent for overturning the whole studio system by separating control of the exhibition, distribution and production branches of the industry. This action was temporarily halted by the war, but was taken up again afterwards, and instituted in 1948. The Paramount decrees broke up the vertically integrated studios, and producers no longer had a guaranteed market for their product. This also had the effect of making the American market appear more vulnerable to British competition.

It had always been a truism that most exhibitors and the mass audience in general in the United States found it very difficult to cultivate a taste for British films, and it was widely thought there that British production values, and specifically the British accent, were a major deterrent. The Board of Trade regularly clipped reviews of British films in the American trade newspapers, and found that these rarely had anything good to say about British feature films. One exhibitor in North Carolina, commenting on *The Adventuress*, wrote in the *Motion Picture Herald*, 'These English pictures are getting very poor. I would hate to think I had to play their pictures to make a living.' Another, reporting on audience reactions to *Stairway to Heaven* in his cinema in Connecticut, wrote, 'The newspapers gave this four stars. My customers gave it four bronx cheers. Color, beautiful. This type might be good for class houses, but they are poison to the guy with the average "thinker". The Board of Trade's researchers agreed that British films only really did well in the United States when they were given a specialized, not a general, release. An exhibitor in California, for example, wrote that *Dead of Night* was 'picked up for a one-night stand and special notice was sent out to art groups, friends of culture and English residents in the country. Their attendance was almost one hundred percent, but due to the fact that hardly anyone else came, business was far below average.'[39]

As these American exhibitors' comments imply, British films as a rule only performed well in the United States before relatively sophisticated audiences, who were reached through the 'art cinema' circuits, or if the films were given special treatment by the distributor and exhibitor. Essentially, virtually all types of British film, whether modest Ealing comedies, or lavish adaptations of Shaw, Dickens or Shakespeare, or documentaries, appealed to very much the same audience. This was identified closely with the type of audience who watched foreign language films in the United States, for whom the 'British accent' posed no problem. The accent which American exhibitors derided so strongly was essentially another foreign language for the mass audience in the United States. In contrast, British films were enjoyed by precisely the same American audiences who would also pay, say, to see the films of Jean Renoir or the Italian neo-realists. Rank films were released in the United States primarily through a special division of Universal called Prestige Pictures. The choice of name for this company left much to be desired. As Richard Griffith noted, this name was 'practically an affront to money-minded distributors and exhibitors. In Hollywood argot, a "prestige" picture is one whose merits may reflect on its producers, but which cannot possibly make money.'[40]

Laurence Olivier's *Henry V* did not receive distribution in the United States until after the war, when it was one of the first British films to receive special handling there. The film waited in American film vaults for over two years while American distributors worked out a marketing campaign. The film was finally released through United Artists, which decided not to sell the film as a movie at all but rather as 'a touring company of the play starring Sir Laurence Olivier'. Paul Lazarus, director of advertising and publicity for United Artists, commented on publicity for this film:

> There was nothing here for regular movie business. But we
> knew we did have something for the devotees of the
> legitimate theatre and for all culturally minded people
> throughout the country. That was the audience we had to
> reach. [41]

The film was released as a roadshow film, carefully advertised and built up in each venue where it opened, with no attempt to immediately aim for the mass market. In the guise of a play, *Henry V* was sent out to college towns, where it was advertised widely and did very well. It was also released in a very calculatedly discriminating fashion to the art cinema circuits. After saturating these markets, the film was then re-launched, targeted this time at wider and more general audiences. The film was shown throughout the United States and eventually grossed more than $4,500,000 there. This seems a good return on one feature film, but, as many critics noted, this was a very expensive way to publicize and distribute a single feature film. *Henry V's* release in the United States became the model campaign for 'quality' British films introduced into the American market. As Arthur Knight noted, *The Red Shoes, Tales of Hoffman, Cyrano De Bergerac* and *Pictura* all imitated the earlier film's marketing campaign in the United States. It appeared as if there was no alternative to this costly form of release if a British film was to do well in the United States.

The Rank Organization was constantly thwarted by its lack of direct control over a major distribution system in the United States. The acquisition of such a system became one of the company's major aims. In 1947, the company began a major offensive into the American market, signalled by a meeting in Britain of the J. Arthur Rank World Film Convention and a subsequent series of conferences there for top Rank executives from all over the world. Rank also merged its American interests with the Eagle-Lion Corporation in order to develop distribution in the United States. It also bought into showcase cinemas in New York and elsewhere in order to debut British films there.

Great Expectations was one of the first British films to be released through this expanded distribution system and ought to have done well in the United States. Unfortunately, its American release coincided with the onset of the Anglo-American film trade war and partly because of widespread and overt hostility to British films in the United States, did fairly poorly at the box office. If anti-British sentiment was not sufficient to sabotage the release of any British film in the United States in 1948, *Great Expectations* suffered from its status as a 'quality' film being retailed in a mass market. The American film audience and film trade did not take to the film, so that 'in the big chains where it played on double bills, attendance was poor; its stars, its title, even its author, meant nothing to the faceless millions who take their movie pabulum from Louella O. Parsons and Hedda Hopper'.[42] In fact, in the plush and cosmopolitan setting of the Radio City Music Hall in New York City, *Great Expectations* actually did extremely well. It played there to good houses for five weeks, and was the first British film to accomplish this since *The Private Life of Henry VIII*. Subsequently, however, the film only played well in long runs at small theatres. What happened to *Great Expectations* and *Hamlet* was symptomatic of the gap between British 'quality' films and the American mass market.

In contrast to the generally decent, if uninspired, performance of 'quality' British films in the American market, mass market British films almost never did very well at the American box office. An exception to this general rule was the reason for the elation of a writer in the British film trade periodical, *Film Industry*, when he heard of the activities of a sympathetic exhibitor in Bethesda, Maryland. This exhibitor ran British film festivals on a regular basis, and he reported good houses for *The Wicked Lady*, *The Rake's Progess* and a revival of *The Ghost Goes West*, all films intended for a mass market in Britain and initially produced with the international market in mind. The Bethesda exhibitor admitted that his festival was fairly unusual because 'distribution of British films in this country is still very spotty. In general most American cinemas still avoid the showing of British films.' [43]

Reaching Agreement

The position of British films in the American market gave the British government little leverage in negotiations with the American film industry. Throughout the winter and spring of 1948, the British government was under great pressure to come to terms with the Motion Picture Association of America. Harold Wilson, at 31 one of the youngest ever Presidents of the Board of Trade, spent much of his tenure at the Board attempting to deal with the films problem. He wanted agreement with the American companies, but also wanted to rehabilitate British film production. Wilson made his position perfectly clear when he introduced the second reading of the Cinematograph Films Act in January 1948. He maintained that Britain needed a strong domestic film industry, both for purposes of

national projection and also for its economic interests. He felt that he
had a strong case because British audiences were far more interested in
British films than they had been before the war. Perhaps being
over-optimistic, he argued:

> If the cinema-going public had the chance today of seeing
> additional British or additional American films, they would
> demand a very much larger number of British films before
> their taste for them was glutted. The day has quite gone
> when one inserted a British film into the programme with an
> apology for doing so. [44]

In this speech in January, Wilson claimed to be unwilling to
compromise. He was not prepared to cave in under the pressure of the
American embargo, nor would he countenance American schemes
whereby American companies would keep a higher proportion of their
British earnings if these were kept inside Britain. He was willing to go
to great lengths to encourage Britain's own film industry. He intended
abolishing producers' and distributors' quotas, whilst raising exhibitors'
quotas to 25%; he also discussed the possibility of both a state-run
film studio and also a state-run bank which would specialize in
guaranteeing funds for film production. In the United States, the film
industry interpreted Wilson's plans very broadly, so that it was
reported: 'Some members of the Motion Picture Association wanted to
placard some extracts from Mr Wilson's speech all over the U.S.A. in
theatres and in newspapers as evidence of an intention to socialise the
film industry.' [45]

Although it was anxious to get earnings from film rentals in
Britain, the American film industry did not feel intimidated by the
actions of the British government and the British film industry. There
was no sudden surge of film production in Britain in early 1948,
despite the promises of Rank and the other British film producers.
Hollywood liked to believe that this failure was a consequence of
government control and militant trade unionism in Britain.
Commenting on the situation in Britain, *Variety* maintained, 'There is
no doubt that the studios' workers have allowed a small noisy clique of
extremists to propagate the belief that with the rationalization of the
industry will come the millenium.' [46] In many ways, this position
was a projection of precisely the types of problems besetting the
American film industry at home. The onset of labour difficulties on a

99

major scale within Hollywood itself, and the industry's own increasingly conservative political stance help explain the American industry's reluctance to deal with a socialist government and also to engage in large-scale production within Britain itself. Inevitably, the industry's own political stance made it hard to come to terms with the British Labour government. In an address appropriately entitled 'Utopia is Production', made after a recent settlement of an industrial dispute, the head of the MPAA had stated the industry's opposition to socialism:

> As we wrestled around in the last round of industrial strife, we
> swayed dangerously close to the cliff of collectivism . . .
> When government starts taking over industry, that is
> collectivism, at least in incipient form. [47]

The American trade press talked of an 'unholy alliance' between J. Arthur Rank and the Labour Party. It also pointed to the financial difficulties of the British film producers as another reason for their failure to increase production: 'British banks have clamped down on making production credits available because of the embargo imposed by American distributors.' [48] This same article also reported on the outcome of a similar American embargo on exporting films to the French film market. There, the government and the industry had essentially capitulated, but the studios' gains had been compromised by a recent devaluation of the French franc, which had substantially reduced the dollar value of film rentals in France. So there was considerable speculation about what would happen if the British pound were devalued also.

The *ad valorem* tax failed completely. Hollywood continued to receive income from those films which had already been in Britain awaiting release prior to the implementation of the tax, and so was relatively cushioned from the immediate effects of the tax. Films made during the embargo were stockpiled for release at a later date. In the short run, the tax brought much more pressure to bear upon British exhibitors and the British government itself than on the American film industry. As spring 1948 approached, so too did the point when there would be no new American films in Britain and in all probability few new British films to show in their place. The poverty of Britain's film industry and its government's film policies were in danger of being exposed.

The Anglo-American Film Agreement

Agreement came in early March 1948, and took the form of virtual capitulation on the part of the British government. In January, Harold Wilson had told the House of Commons: 'I am sure I can say to Hollywood that if they believe they can squeeze us into modifying our attitude on the duty by continuing the embargo, they are backing a loser.' [49] Unfortunately, this is precisely what happened, and the form the agreement assumed was also one which Wilson had repeatedly claimed would never be acceptable. Under the terms of the Anglo-American Film Agreement, which would take effect in June 1948, the government made many concessions. American producers would be allowed to distribute a total of 180 American feature films in the British market. They would also be allowed to take up to a total of £17,000,000 of their earnings out of the country, with the balance of their revenues to be re-invested in Britain. It was estimated that if American film revenues in Britain stayed at their 1947 level, some £10,000,000 would be frozen in Britain each year, with no more than £1,250,000 of this to be invested outside the British film industry. [50] In addition, American producers would be able to increase the earnings they took out of Britain by an amount equivalent to the earnings of British feature films in the American market. The Board of Trade argued that this new agreement gave the Americans an incentive to develop the market for British films in the United States and also tapped the frozen assets in Britain as a source of potential investment capital for the financially strapped British film industry.

The American film industry was not overjoyed with the new settlement, despite the fact that a leader in the *Daily Express* maintained that the agreement was out-and-out victory for the MPAA and humiliation for Britain. Producers in Hollywood believed that they lost a great deal with the agreement, specifically, it placed a ceiling on the proportion of their earnings which they could take out of Great Britain. As the President of Loews International noted, 'Negotiations should justifiably have resulted in a more equitable agreement, (but) we are all happy that the cause of discord has been dissipated.' [51] On the other hand, in Britain, there was widespread concern that the frozen American assets would be the basis for an eventual takeover of the British film industry.

British exhibitors, for their part, eagerly awaited the conclusion of the 'film famine'. The Anglo-American Agreement was scheduled to take effect from 14 June 1948. Exhibitors' eagerness pointed to the essentially colonial nature of American control of the British film industry and the British film audience - both had conspired against the dictates of their own government. National economic policy might require that precious dollars go to pay for necessities, but ultimately it was found that so far as the rank and file of the British cinema audience was concerned, American films were a necessity.

Notes

1. G. M. Mayer, 'American Motion Pictures in World Trade', *Annals of the American Academy of Political and Social Science*, no. 254, (1947), p. 31.
2. 'Notes on Films for the British Embassy in Washington D.C.', October 1948, BT 11/3687.
3. C. Steinberg, *Film Facts* , (Facts on Film, New York, 1980), p. 85.
4. N. D. Golden and E. H. Young, 'World Survey Shows Record Foreign Business for U.S. Films', *Foreign Commerce Weekly*, 28 February 1955, unpaged reprint.
5. 'Notes about the Film Industry', October, 1948, BT 64/2292.
6. R. Manvell, *Film*, (Penguin, London, 1944, revised 1950 edition), p. 136.
7. Stafford Cripps, 'Films' memorandum, 19 November, 1945, BT 64/2188
8. A.C.T. memorandum for the Portal Committee, 5 January, 1949, BT 64/2426.
9. *Variety*, 16 January 1985.
10. *The Times*, 11 July 1947.
11. F. D. Klingender and S. Legg, *Money Behind the Screen* (Film Centre, London, 1937), p. 83, noted that between 1925 and 1935, the number of film production companies registered in Britain rose from 15 to 108.
12. H. L. French, Director-General, British Film Producers Association, *The Times*, 15 June 1948

13. F.W. Allport, European Manager Motion Picture Association of America, *The Times*, 29 June 1948. Allport used figures from the Board of Trade Journal.
14. Hansard, column 143, 2 July 1947.
15. Memorandum on meeting attended by Sir John Magowen, Sir Wilfred Eady, Eric Johnston and Allen Dulles, 23 August 1947, BT 64/2283.
16. G. H. Gallup (ed.), *The Gallup International Public Opinion Polls, Great Britain, 1937 - 1975*, (Random House, New York, 1976).
17. Hansard, column 2541, 16 November 1945.
18. Introduction, *Kine Year Book*, 1948.
19. At the British Public Records Office, there is a large file devoted exclusively to 'Schemes for Limitations of Film Remittances to the United States'.
20. Hansard, column 2539, 16 November 1945.
21. N. D. Golden, 'Future of U.S. Pix Abroad Grave As Curbs Pile Up', *Variety*, 7 January 1948.
22. *The Times*, 23 April 1947.
23. Parker to Shacke, British Delegation, International Trade Organization, 12 May 1947, BT 64/2283.
24. For an interesting recent account of Rank's negotiations with the American market, see R. Murphy, 'Rank's Attempt on the American Market, 1944-9', in J. Curran and V. Porter (eds.), *British Cinema History* (Weidenfeld and Nicolson, London, 1983), pp. 164-78.
25. *New York Times*, 9 August 1947.
26. *Ibid.*, 11 August 1947.
27. *Variety*, 7 January 1948.
28. E. Johnston, *We're All In It* (E. P. Dutton, New York, 1948), pp. 23-4.
29. Golden, 'Future of U.S. Pix'
30. Munro to Inverchapel, 28 August 1947, BT 64/2283.
31. Minute, 'U.K. Films Tax', 10 February 1948, BT 64/2370.
32. *Today's Cinema*, 14 August 1947.
33. D. Catling, 'The Independent Frame', *Film Industry*, February (1948), pp. 7 - 20. Darrel Catling was the director of *Under the Frozen Falls*, the first film to be made using the independent frame

34. *Variety*, 7 January 1948.
35. *New York Times*, 4 April 1948.
36. Gallup, *Gallup International*, The poll was taken in September 1947.
37. *Caesar and Cleopatra* was a notoriously extravagant film. At a time when the typical British film cost approximately £100,000 to £150,000, it was rumoured to have cost in excess of £1,000,000.
38. R. Griffith, 'Where are the Dollars ? 1' *Sight and Sound*, December (1949), pp. 33 - 4.
39. Board of Trade clippings file, BT 64/2366.
40. Griffith, 'Where are the Dollars ? 1'
41. A. Knight, 'The Reluctant Audience', *Sight and Sound*, vol. 22, no. 4 (1953), pp. 191-2.
42. R. Griffith, 'Where are the Dollars ? 2', *Sight and Sound*, January 1950, pp. 39 - 40.
43. 'Here's How One American Exhibitor Sells British Pictures', *Film Industry*, October 1947.
44. Harold Wilson, Hansard, column 219, 21 January 1948.
45. Minute, 'U.K. Films Tax'.
46. *Variety*, 7 January 1948.
47. E. Johnston, 'Utopia is Production', an address to the Convention of the International Alliance of Theatrical Stage Managers and Motion Picture Machine Operators, 23 July 1946.
48. *Variety*, 28 January 1948.
49. Wilson, Hansard.
50. *Kine Weekly*, 18 March 1948.
51. *Ibid.*

Chapter Seven

US Cultural Policy in Postwar Britain

> Especially in the postwar period, the (State) Department desires
> to cooperate fully in the protection of American motion
> pictures abroad. It expects in return that the industry will co-
> operate wholeheartedly with the government with a view to in-
> suring that the pictures distributed abroad will reflect credit on
> the good name and reputation of this country and its
> institutions. [1]

> If the United States abolished its diplomatic and consular
> services, kept its ships in its harbours, and tourists at home
> and retired from the world markets, its citizens, its problems,
> its towns and countryside, its roads, its motor cars, eating
> houses and saloons would still be familiar in the utmost
> corners of the world. The film is to America what the flag once
> was to Great Britain. [2]

This chapter is an examination of some of the cultural policies
pursued overtly by the American government in postwar Britain, and
specifically the relationship between the US government and the US
film industry and their collusion overseas. Special attention is given to
the commercial and official bodies created by the government and the
film industry for this work overseas, the Motion Picture Export
Association and the International Media Guaranty Program.

A special problem, and perhaps the most important issue, for the
United States government and for Americans in general in their
dealings with postwar Britain was the peculiar strain of
anti-Americanism which surfaced there during and after the war, and
this became a significant factor in the conduct of Anglo-American
relations during the postwar decade. This became especially relevant
when American public opinion mounted against specific British

policies, as in its actions in Palestine, and when the United States tried to commit England to large-scale involvement overseas, particularly the war in Korea. Unsurprisingly perhaps, several influential members of the Hollywood community were deeply involved in the Zionist cause and campaigned actively against British policies in Palestine. Similarly, the Korean war, which was a very expensive conflict for Britain, and led to a very perceptible, albeit temporary, decline in the British standard of living, was very unpopular with the British general public, and was a real source of antagonism between the British and the United States.

Britain had a unique relationship with the United States after the Second World War. Britain could not have sustained its involvement in the war without extensive aid from the United States. In fact, as early as the beginning of 1941 Britain's own financial resources had evaporated and it was only 'thanks to lend-lease that Great Britain kept up a misleading appearance as a Great Power until almost the end of the war'. [3] Britain was therefore extremely dependent upon the financial resources of the United States, which sometimes chose to support the illusion that Britain remained a great power, and sometimes not. Britain was not a client nation in quite the same way that many other powers were, but it was widely felt both within Britain and the United States that American aid had purchased a huge amount of influence over Britain's internal and overseas affairs. Yet at the same time most British people were at a loss as to how this could have come about:

> In the hour of victory there were very few who could
> understand the extent of Britain's financial nudity...Ordinary
> people could not understand that a winning power at the head
> of a great empire, apparently second only to the United States
> in influence, could be destitute. [4]

Britain was neither a defeated nation nor one of those states which had suffered from occupation by the Axis powers during the war. Nevertheless, in contrast to the supercharging effect which the war had had upon the American economy, Britain's own economy had been seriously weakened by the war, and the overseas reserves which had acted as a barrier for the British people for so many years had all but disappeared. In this respect, the British film industry was an anomaly. It had benefited in many ways from the war, and, if anything, peacetime encouraged the film industry to have unrealistic expectations for the future. In other ways, the history of the postwar British film industry was very typical of what happend to British industry then, in the growth of government regulation and control, increasing reliance upon public funding, and an attempt to help the balance of payments by producing with an eye on the overseas market. It took a long period of adjustment for the British to appreciate the changes in the two countries' relative standing.

Britain lacked both the military and the financial clout to still be a 'great power' and yet it was equally evident that the U.S.A. needed Britain to counterbalance the Soviet Union's expansion into Eastern Europe. It was inconceivable that the U.S.A. and Britain could survive as equal partners as they had been before and during the war, and yet the status of 'junior partner' rankled with the British.

Anti-Americanism or resentment of Americans, as Fred Vanderschmidt noted, was a regular feature of newspaper reporting after the war. Don Iddon, New York columnist for the *Daily Mail*, wrote a weekly column which was frequently scathing of American insensitivity and ingratitude towards the British. A suggestion that Britain's transatlantic fleet be sold off to help pay off war debts caused him to respond:

> Several souls have suggested we sell the Queen Mary and
> Queen Elizabeth to raise money. Better live on bread and water
> than sell them. What a delightful reward for victory, and
> holding off America's enemy alone for a year, that would be. [5]

In fact, the British newspapers were regularly full of acrimonious reports of this sort, which often focused upon the differences in living standards and expectations between the Americans and the British, and which in some way seemed unfair in view of the debt which most British people felt Americans owed to them for their part in the war. The author of a column in the trade newspaper, *World's Press News*, represented the opinions of probably the majority of British journalists when he noted, 'We think it ironic that the mere 48,000,000 of us who saved the entire civilised world in 1940 should now be rewarded by being on the rocks'. [6]

The United States government had great influence with the British government, which went beyond mere control of the international purse strings. Postwar Britain lived under the 'nuclear umbrella' created by the Americans, and relied heavily upon US aid to fulfil its obligations overseas. This military and financial interdependence was fundamentally very different from anything the British had ever experienced before. Furthermore, there were some grounds for mutual animosity between the British and the Americans. Ideologically, President Truman, to a much greater extent than his predecessor, was hostile to the Labour government's socialism and commitment to a planned nationalized economy. Furthermore, most Americans were fairly critical of British foreign policy, particularly in the case of Palestine. For their part, the British government and the British people were disturbed by the purchasing power of the dollar - as was the world as a whole. Despite all this, the two governments worked surprisingly well together, especially when once again, during the Berlin Airlift, Korea and the Cold War, they had a common enemy to drive them into each other's arms.

It is difficult to ascertain the nature of the influence which the American government was able to consciously exert and control over the British people as opposed to the British government. It is almost always harder to document popular appeal than ministerial minutes. Nevertheless, there is a considerable quantity of material relating to the activities of the American government attempting to sway not just the British, but many other European nations too. The US government was always faced by a dilemma in its dealings with the British public. It was confronted by a surprisingly virulent anti-Americanism. Fred Vanderschmidt maintained that this was principally a device used by the *Daily Mirror* and other popular dailies to increase circulations, and that it became a bandwagon joined by many aspiring politicians. Whether evidenced in public opinion polls, or in more openly and obviously expressed hostility to American visitors, there were frequent instances of anti-Americanism in the postwar decade. Yet at the same time, and often amongst the very same people who were so hostile, the 'American way' retailed by G.I.s, motion pictures, and practically all forms of popular culture had a great appeal to wide sections of the British public. There was a contradiction here whose resolution was in some respects central to American cultural policy in Great Britain.

Britain and the United States fought the last three months of the Second World War under new leaders. Harry Truman had served as a vice president, little thinking, like everybody else, that he would be the president himself one day. Truman was in many ways the quintessential smalltown middle American business politician. He was reputed to get up at 6.00 every morning to walk around the White House, greeting all those he saw. His demeanour and world view were very different from those of the anglophile patrician, Franklin Roosevelt. Few people knew exactly what to expect when Truman assumed power, but everybody assumed that he would adopt a businesslike if somewhat parochial attitude towards foreign policy. [7] Eisenhower was also a typically American leader, though not from Truman's 'business as usual' school of thinking. Neither of them was as solicitous towards Britain as Roosevelt had been. Also, both faced the emergence of a divided Europe and expansionist communism, and both were the leaders of the West in a way that Roosevelt was not. The United States they led was a superpower to an extent it had not been under Roosevelt.

The British astonished the British Conservative Party and also the United States by ousting Churchill and the Conservatives in the 1945 general election. Until then, it seemed as if the Conservatives had acquired the status of natural governing party. Either on its own, or as the senior partner in a series of national governments, the Conservative Party had ruled Britain for over fifteen years. Furthermore, the Conservative Party had expected to profit from Churchill's own great personal prestige. In fact, Churchill's own reputation stood very high at the end of the war, but, if the Conservatives had paid any attention to a number of opinion polls taken during the war, they would have been aware that the British public wanted a change from the old policies to which the Conservatives were irrevocably wedded. In fact, the overwhelming victory by the Labour Party in the 1945 general election was essentially guaranteed by the social and political changes precipitated by the prewar depression and the war itself. The conflict had evolved into a genuine 'people's war' and had a very democratizing effect on the ways in which the war was conducted and British society organized itself. Although, as Paul Addison has recently noted, 'War did not revolutionize the British, but it radicalised them. There was never a serious prospect that the social structure would collapse.' [8] The war succeeded in politicizing many people to an extent unthought of before the war. Few ordinary working people were prepared to return to the conditions which had prevailed before 1939. Many Labour Party leaders had demonstrated their administrative ability as members of the

109

national government during the war, so that, as never before, they seemed a realistic alternative to the Conservatives. The Labour Party also benefited from the widespread belief that the massive successes of the Red Army during the war had proved the advantages of the planned economy. [9] Consequently, there was a very concerted effort at the ballot box to vote in a party which would continue the major policy and planning changes instituted during the war.

The Labour victory was a genuine mystery for many Americans for whom the half American Churchill had personified British resistance. The rejection of Churchill was seen as an act of ingratitude towards a great wartime leader. Others had a more sinister interpretration of the Labour victory, which they saw as the beginning of creeping socialism, and the emergence of a planned economy which would compete with American-style free enterprise.

America After Yalta

The Yalta conference was the first attempt by the United States to reshape the map of Europe and to carve for itself a sphere of influence within Europe. Truman and his advisors had not anticipated that Soviet Russia would go beyond a 'sphere of influence' policy in Eastern Europe to erect a series of satellite regimes there. Consequently, US policy evolved into the straightforward decision to buttress up Western Europe against Eastern aggression. Britain's junior status in the arrangement with the United States was very clear. The British Isles were to be transformed into an unsinkable atomic aircraft carrier for the American airforce. Gradually the United States accepted responsibility for some of Britain's commitments in Europe. In February 1947, Truman invoked the 'Truman Doctrine' when taking over from Britain during the crisis in Greece. Britain learnt to always yield to American policies in Germany, and the two worked together during the Berlin Airlift, from July 1948 until May 1949. All these actions in the Cold War culminated in the creation of NATO in April 1949.

Anglo-American relations were obviously a very crucial issue on both sides of the Atlantic, giving rise in each country to a wide range of opinions about the prospects for this relationship. In the United States, the traditionally widespread scepticism regarding 'perfidious Albion' survived, reinforced in some respects by the experiences of many American GIs stationed in Britain. George Orwell, for example, had returned repeatedly to the question of the mutual hostility of the British and Americans stationed in Britain in his wartime journalism, noting 'it is difficult to go anywhere in London without having the feeling that Britain is now Occupied Territory', and the extent to which Americans and Britons had become alienated from each other largely on account of this semi-colonial situation. [10] In particular, in the United States, there was a widespread and barely suppressed hostility towards the British ruling elite. In fact, it was this hostility to the accents of the West End which partially accounted for the failure of British films in the United States. Perhaps these prejudices did the most harm during negotiations for successive American loans - the British ruling elite protested loudly about becoming so indebted to the United States. In fact, the formal discussions for American loans were often stifled by the complete lack of rapport between the downhome populist, Fred Vinson, Secretary of the Treasury, and the urbane intellectual, John Maynard Keynes.

The 49th State

British people reciprocated the widespread American hostility towards themselves. Again, the American 'occupation' of Britain prior to the invasion of Europe had not endeared America to the general public in Britain. The American army's presence reiterated the lessons given by American motion pictures, and concretized all those fantasies in lots of ways, but there is much evidence that the American army also engendered a lot of hostility on both sides. In fact, a series of Mass Observation surveys undertaken during and immediately after the war in Britain showed that Russia was consistently much more popular with the British public than the United States. [11] After all, during the war, the British saw lots of relatively inactive G.I.s in Britain whilst they saw many references in the newsreels and in the headlines to the gallant Red Army's struggle against the Germans. Immediately after the war, Mass Observation found that, although the extent of British approval for Russia began to slip, there was also 'an alarming increase in anti-Americanism'. In particular, it was found that American policy on Palestine, its intervention in Greece and Turkey, and the introduction of Marshall Aid had the greatest impact upon British public opinion. American loans were tied to US foreign policy in some fairly complex ways. As the British Embassy in Washington D.C. reported, concerning the renewal of American aid to Britain after the withdrawal of Lend-Lease: 'The main propulsive force

111

behind the loan is felt to be none other than Stalin, whose tactics have created a greater volume of sentiment in favour of support for Britain than our own unaided efforts could probably ever have achieved.' [12]

After the war, US actions, especially in the areas of giving and withholding financial aid, generated more hostility and suspicion, which crossed lines of social class. Business people and many right wing politicians commonly believed that the United States was using its economic power to humble and colonize its former ally. Lord Rotherwyck, speaking to the British Chamber of Shipping, maintained that begging for American loans was 'nothing more or less than the selling of the British Empire and its independence to America'. [13] It was often maintained by people of this persuasion that Britain was being reduced to the standing of a '49th state', a phrase which was used frequently at the time. Underlying this position was the notion that Britain's postwar economic plight was primarily the fault of the United States, which owed its wartime ally so much, and had a clear vested interest in its rehabilitation. On the other hand, there were some Conservative commentators, like Virginia Cowles, who thought that, on the whole, the British were very grateful to the United States for financing their postwar recovery. In *No Cause For Alarm*, a work intended primarily for an American readership, she argued that there was little that was taking place in postwar Britain that was very radical, and that ultimately a reinvigorated Tory democracy would assume power there. In the interim, she maintained that the British did not resent their increasing dependence upon the United States. As she put it:

> The fact that America is subsidising Britain to the tune of six
> shillings a week per family is well known to the British
> people. And this generally is not taken for granted. British
> people feel deeply indebted to America, and instead of
> disliking their creditor, a practice which is usually regarded as
> inevitable, friendship for the United States has never been
> firmer, or gratitude more genuine. 14

The Left in Britain took a rather less clearly divided position - and its views had a ready ear in the Labour Party. For many, US actions in postwar Europe were easily interpreted as the inevitable consequences of predatory capitalism. American loans were merely another means of extending American control into Britain. Americans for their part were more than willing to assume that the British labour movement had been infiltrated by communists who looked to Russia for leadership, though usually resentment rather than ideology was regarded as the mainspring of anti-Americanism. After hearing a series of anti-American speeches at the 1947 Trades Union Congress Fred Vanderschmidt commented :

> I realise there are powerful Communist influences in the British trades unions - considerably more powerful than in British politics, and quite openly so. But this was more than a Communist clique. It was the pent-up resentment of the have-not and ought-to-have workers against the successful capitalism three thousand miles across that sea. [15]

The United States had to face a permanent retreat from its traditional isolationist stance. There was no possibility that America could turn its back on the rest of the world, as it had done in many ways after the First World War. Historically, Britain had policed the world as a part of the British Empire's historic destiny, or, again, for the more cynical, out of a quest for colonial gain, and this was the mantle which the United States had to assume. The US felt obliged to accept responsibility for reconstructing the postwar world, including in large measure Europe itself. The British Empire posed special problems for the United States. Here too, the US felt that holding the purse strings entitled it to make its views known.

On both sides of the Atlantic, it was also often assumed that American aid would entail some degree of American control over Britain's internal and external affairs. As Andre Visson noted:

> Of all western European nations, none feels itself closer to America than the British; none is more aware of its unswerving solidarity with the United States; and none is more alarmed, more irritated and more unhappy whenever its people have - or believe they have - reason to suspect that this solidarity takes on the character of dependence. [16]

In retrospect, the British and US governments had a relatively good working relationship despite one's perpetual mendicancy and the other's reluctant philanthropy. It is easy to see expediency at work here, especially after the onset of the Cold War, but nevertheless what emerges is that the two governments thought much more highly of each other than did the respective populations of the two countries.

America could not plan the rehabilitation of the British economy in the way in which it could renew the national economies of Japan and Germany. Britain had sold off many of the overseas investments that had made it possible for the country to have a perennial visible balance of payments deficit. Henceforth, Britain's own manufacturing economy would have to generate sufficient manufactures to pay the nation's import (food) bill - something it had not done since before the First World War. Yet, there is little question that the United States was fairly hostile to the notion of a planned British economy in peacetime. A centralized and planned economy might be necessary in wartime, but in other circumstances it threatened to interfere with the free flow of American dollars and trade.

The American Film Industry and the US Government

Motion pictures are an interesting export item. In contrast to most manufactures, they cost relatively little to export, making few demands for shipping, storage and subsequent distribution. Furthermore, once initial negative costs are paid back, after distribution and publicity costs, the balance of receipts is largely profit.

As noted in a previous chapter, the American government was surprisingly uncooperative in its dealings with the Motion Picture Export Association on the matter of the American embargo, preferring to support the reconstruction efforts of the British government over those of its own film industry - at least in this one instance. It felt at that time that it was more important to support the British government's economic reconstruction policies than to support the immediate commercial concerns of its own film industry. Nevertheless, when the film industry could create at least the pretence that it was working in the national interest, rather than out of self-interest, it could expect, and usually received, a great deal of co-operation from the United States government.

Hollywood's publicists and the inevitably conspicuous nature of the American feature film have done much to distort and inflate our sense of the true net worth of the Hollywood feature film in overseas trade. Compared to other types of US export, both industrial and financial, the feature film has never ranked at the top of American overseas exports. Although as Eric Johnston, President of the MPEA reported in an annual report in the mid-fifties:

> In view of the motion picture industry's tremendous export
> business, representing in terms of the proportion of total sales,
> the largest export industry of any size in the United States, the
> course of United States trade policy is of more than academic
> interest . . . it is the only large film industry in the world
> which is not directly or indirectly subsidised or supported by
> government. [17]

Nevertheless, films have been an important part of the United
States' overall revenues from overseas trade, particularly because of the
peculiar circumstances in which they are sold overseas and also because
of their inevitable multiplier effect - the way in which films, as John
Grierson put it, have served as 'indirect publicity' for the goods and
services produced by the United States. Equally important, overseas
receipts have always been very important to the film industry itself,
since films were often budgeted on the assumption that ultimately they
would receive revenues from the overseas markets.

There were special circumstances surrounding the American film
industry in the postwar decade which made overseas sales particularly
important. The decline of domestic revenues made the overseas box
office disproportionately important, and British receipts were often in
excess of 60% of the total overseas take. Hollywood had been denied
markets in occupied Europe during the war, and had been waiting to
expand back into the market when peace was declared. The industry
also had a very optimistic view of the future fuelled by the dramatic
expansion of the American film market during the war. When domestic
demand shrank in the years immediately following the war, Hollywood made even more demands on the overseas markets. In 1937, the
US Department of Commerce reported that 40% of the income of the
motion picture industry came from overseas sales. Twenty years later,
various figures for revenues from film rentals overseas were noted,
ranging from a figure of 43% of the studios' total earnings, cited in
the *New York Times* in February 1958, to a figure of over 50%
quoted in the *Morning Telegraph* six months later. Interestingly
enough, the MPEA's own official publications at this time were fairly
vague about the precise figures for overseas sales. Its 1955 annual
report stated only that 'vigorous and steady growth has been the
keynote of the American motion picture industry's international

business during the past decade'.

Motion pictures first became a major export item for the US in the 1920s, and it was then that the Department of Commerce began to produce special surveys of the international market for films as part of its regular market intelligence service. In 1926 the Department of Commerce created a special motion picture division within the Electrical Products Division of the Bureau of Foreign and Domestic Commerce. Its work included proselytizing for the American film overseas, but its primary task was supplying Hollywood with information about overseas markets. In July 1937, a Motion Picture Division was established at the bureau, headed by the chief of the earlier body, Nathan Golden. When announcing the creation of the new department, the Secretary of Commerce alluded to the significance of feature films as overseas advertisement:

> According to Alexander V. Dye, director of the Board of
> Foreign and Domestic Commerce, goods shown in the
> American movies, such as American household articles,
> automobiles, industrial machinery, clothing and many other
> items, owe much of their popularity abroad to the fact that
> millions see them in the pictures. [18]

The Motion Picture Division made regular reports concerning the attempts of foreign governments to regulate film imports. Generally, Britain led the way in attempting different techniques to limit film imports and to challenge the supremacy of Hollywood. The Division's lengthy 1936 report, for example, noted that the findings of the Moyne Committee in Britain and the use of quota legislation there were a consequence of 'a very intensive national feeling that American habits of speech, dress, and local customs may become widely adopted in Great Britain'. [19]

There has been a long tradition of co-operation amongst the different studios on industrial and policy matters, and also a willingness to establish central regulatory bodies, especially if this removed the necessity of regulation by outside bodies. The Motion Picture Association of America, for example, had been established as a form of self-regulation by the industry, and it had seemed completely appropriate to appoint as its first head a former Republican Cabinet official, Will B. Hays. Subsequently, in 1945, under the terms of the Webb-Pomerene Act, which permitted trust arrangements geared to overseas markets, the film industry established its own overseas sales bureau, the Motion Picture Export Association. [20] The film trade was very optimistic about prospects for the MPEA: 'Although there has been considerable talk off and on about a united front for operations in foreign lands, this is the first time the American film industry actually has set up the machinery for a united front.' [21] The MPEA played an important role in negotiating on behalf of the American motion picture industry with foreign governments. Initially, it was primarily concerned with representing member company distributors in countries disrupted or devastated by the war and selling films to state-controlled film monopolies, especially those associated with the Soviet Union's sphere of influence. It was reorganized in 1953 to assume responsibility for all the overseas activities of its members. [22]

The US government was in something of a quandary in its dealings with the MPEA. At home, the government had resumed the lawsuit against Paramount which was destined ultimately to strip all the studios of their monopoly powers and separate the different branches of the film industry. It recognized the contradiction in doing this whilst at the same time the MPEA was encouraging monopoly action overseas: 'At a time when the stress of United States public policy in regard to the motion picture industry as an economic affair is upon the need for competition, flexibility and individuality, there are limits to the extent to which the government could afford to stimulate concert of action in relation to the foreign market.' [23]

1946 was the best year of business in the domestic market which Hollywood ever experienced. The year following was one of the worst. In the United States, the number of average weekly admissions dropped by almost one half from 90 million in 1946 to 46.5 million in 1956. [24] Although people still continued to spend a very high proportion of their income on cinema, other forms of leisure began to compete with Hollywood for their purchasing power. In essence, the film industry faced important demographic and sociological changes which led leisure activities to become much more family-centred. As films lost their hold on the American family, which began to happen even prior to the introduction of television on a large scale in the United States, films increasingly adopted forms and content appropriate to an adolescent audience.

The film industry became so aggressive selling its output overseas because receipts from overseas often were the difference between profit and loss. However, the world over, national governments reacted to the dollar crisis by trying to restrict the number of American films entering their borders. In a sense, this led to greater state intervention in the dealings of the American film industry, on the part of both foreign governments and also the United States government. A decade earlier, Walter Wanger had argued that foreign governments had much too much influence with Hollywood producers, who were anxious to tailor representations for foreign nations to the desires of foreign governments. He believed that the German government and other foreign powers had greater influence upon the American film industry than the US government had:

> The habit of bowing to every domestic critic prepared it (the film industry) to be subservient abroad whenever a foreign market seemed threatened. The relationship of the American motion picture industry to foreign markets and to foreign governments has had two other interesting characteristics: (a) Foreign governments have strongly resisted what they consider a trade invasion as well as an invasion of ideas. (b) The American government has failed to give support, or at least has given ineffectual support, against foreign discriminations and trade barriers set up especially to restrict or stop the distribution of American films. This is a natural extension into the foreign field of the industry's domestic policy of surrendering to almost any sort of objection, criticism or threat. [25]

It might be argued that this was very much a prewar position, but there is no doubt that many lobbyists continued to maintain that foreign governments had too much influence with their own government on film matters even after the war. Siegfried Kracauer, for example, noted the manner in which films were vetted by foreign governments in order to prevent slurs against other races and nations. Kracauer noted that this was part of the on-going 'Tensions Project' begun by UNESCO after the war, which examined motion pictures and other forms of mass media, trying to assess 'the conceptions which the people of one nation entertain of their own and of other nations'. [26] UNESCO was closely tied to United States cultural policy and so was especially concerned with the representation of the United States overseas.

118

The American government and the American film industry traditionally were very close. Their friendship had grown during the war, when the Office of War Information and the studios had worked together in the production of theatrical and non-theatrical material for the war effort. In addition, the American government had come to appreciate the extent to which the American motion picture functioned as trade and ideological advertisement. Again, this was something perhaps most clearly stated in the United States by film producers like Walter Wanger:

Trade follows the film. American automobile sales increase when foreign communities see some favorite American star riding around in an attractive new model car. Back in silent picture days a wholesale appliance house in Athens, Greece, cabled for thirty barber chairs 'like the one in the picture.' The stimulus sometimes has an almost 'revolutionary' result. A strike of Paris stenographers once was laid to the influence of films which showed how much better equipment, sanitation, light and air were enjoyed as a matter of course by office-workers in this country. [27]

Each year, the Office of International Trade at the Department of Commerce filed reports on the overseas markets for the motion picture. The reports on the United Kingdom for 1948 and 1949 noted the ways in which the dollar crisis and growing government restrictions were making it increasingly difficult to deal with the British market, although, since this was still much the biggest market Hollywood possessed, it was vital to deal with all these restrictions. The commercial attache in London noted:

The largest 1948 box office draw in the country was a United States feature; second place was accorded a British feature. Of the top 15 box office attractions in 1948, 9 were British films and 6 were from the United States . . . . It is believed that an Englishman enjoys or dislikes United States films for the same reasons as does an American, and although there had been much criticism of United States films during 1948 the public continues to heavily patronise the majority of United States films shown. It is generally believed that most movie audiences prefer films which have important stars in them, whereas more sophisticated London audiences may prefer films whose value rests in the theme and method of its presentation. According to a survey of movie-going habits in Britain made in 1947, a high proportion of movie goers exercise little choice as regards the films they see.

It is impossible to give specific instances where United States pictures have been responsible for the sale of United States merchandise in the British market. With existing regulations restricting importation of merchandise from hard-currency areas the part played by United States motion pictures in prompting sales is hard to determine. It is felt that an interest is created in United States household appliances, clothing styles, and automobiles by the showing of United States films. United States motion pictures are one of the most effective channels still open for keeping United States goods before the public during the time when only small amounts of United States goods can be imported. [28]

It was widely believed on both sides of the Atlantic that American feature films in postwar Britain were a potent means to create demand and engender consumerism.

At home, the American film industry began trying to prove its own loyalty and patriotism. Friendly witnesses made appearances before the House Un-American Activities Committee, suspected communist sympathizers and fellow travellers were blacklisted, and in many other ways the industry began to indulge in self-immolation. This has been thoroughly discussed in a number of recent studies written from a variety of perspectives. [29] Unsurprisingly, the fight against communism found its way into the actual content of the films produced in Hollywood, though the evidence suggests that the more blatant forms of anti-communist propaganda tended to do very poorly at the commercial box office. The motion picture industry was anxious to appear ultra-patriotic; its fight against communism, begun during the war and now in full swing, made it very wary of any signs of communist encroachment - or for that matter 'socialist experiment' overseas.

In other ways, too, the Hollywood community attempted to shape American foreign policy. The issue which was the flashpoint for Britain and a number of senior people in the film industry was Palestine. Zionist sympathizers in Hollywood like Ben Hecht attempted to rally public opinion against British actions in Palestine, very much in the way that Irish-Americans call for the withdrawal of British troops from Northern Ireland today. Hecht and others took out full page advertisements in the New York Times and other quality newspapers to campaign against the British. In many ways, Palestine and a fairly open anti-semitism in Britain were a major problem in the conduct of Anglo-American relations. As Fred Vanderschmidt put it: 'Basically, the attitude which some Americans have taken toward British travail in Palestine has served to cement the traditional British conviction that we do not have stability, or responsibility, that we cannot be trusted to think and act with maturity and wisdom, and that our relations with the rest of the world are dictated alternatively by our emotions or by our self interest. [30]

The United States government did not attempt to orchestrate British public opinion on Palestine. This was probably just as well, since opinion polls from the period indicate an astonishing lack of knowledge about foreign affairs amongst the British public. Nevertheless, amongst British journalists, and, it is reasonable to suggest, within the political establishment as well, there was a great deal of hostility towards the United States, and this was especially directed against 'the Wall Street Jews and their debased hirelings - Ben Hecht, Louis Bromfield and others of that highly odorous crowd'. [31] Divergent American and British interests in the Middle East would culminate in the British disaster and humiliation over Suez.

The US State Department was very conscious of the value of cultural projection overseas. A memorandum written immediately after the war drew attention to America's overwhelming control of the overseas film market, and claimed that it was ironic that the government did not in any direct way control the image of the United States sold overseas in motion pictures and other popular forms:

> The same big pictures are made for both domestic and foreign showings. One result of the overlap is that, even if by increased awareness and self-criticism the stereotypes or allusions that particularly offend other peoples can be eliminated (and the prospects for such elimination are bright), the pictures might still present to other societies what would seem to them a tawdry picture of the United States. In other words, it may be easier to get rid of insults to other countries than damage to the reputation of the United States. [32]

The memorandum questioned the government's ability to control the content and effect of feature films, and maintained that a balanced impression - 'balance' was always the stated objective - would be aided considerably by the use of non-theatrical films. The report took a position astonishingly similar to that first presented to the British government by John Grierson over twenty years previously. It maintained that 'educational and cultural 16 mm films' would act as 'continuous antidotes to many of our commercial pictures'. One correspondent answering a recent State Department's questionnaire on American motion pictures in the postwar world thought 16 mm non-theatrical films 'should correct the current overemphasis upon bigness, power, and mechanised energy and the underemphasis upon good material products'.

The memorandum proposed a central government film office which would commisson film productions for distribution overseas, and subsequently, in 1946, the Division of International Motion Pictures was created within the State Department. In one unique respect, the United States had greater problems in projecting itself overseas via documentary films than most other countries. As Robert Katz put it, this was because such films had to reach 'audiences whose visual concept of the United States has been firmly established by Hollywood feature productions, most of which, according to Walter White, are often referred to as 'American kiss-kiss, bang-bang pictures'. [33] Significantly, the IMP never achieved its objectives. It suffered from budget cuts within a year of its inception and never succeeded in reaching a large audience. Significantly, Katz made very favourably references to the work of the National Film Board of Canada and the film service of the British Library of Information in New York, hoping that the IMP could be as efficient as they were. In other words, this was an American recommending that the US government emulate the Griersonian tradition of government-sponsored documentary film production, which had itself grown out of a rejection of the American feature film.

Starting in 1948, the US government embarked on a major programme of cultural projection overseas with its Informational Media Guaranty Program. It aimed to facilitate the export of all cultural forms and educational materials, including the sale of American books, magazines, newspapers and motion pictures overseas, by guaranteeing that exporters would be paid in dollars for their sales even in those countries where local currencies were not freely convertible. After the 1948 Anglo-American Film Agreement, Britain was the market where the largest proportion of earnings for the American film industry overseas were not freely convertible, since under the terms of the agreement the American studios were only able to withdraw a portion of their total earnings in the United Kingdom to the value of $17,000, 000. [34]

Locating specific examples of either the United States government or the American film industry consciously using individual motion pictures within Britain to lobby there for specific foreign policy objectives, or more generally, against the Labour government's plans for nationalization and a planned economy is perhaps to miss the point. The essential ideology retailed in virtually all American feature films was so markedly different from that in those films produced in Britain during the same period that they offered not just opportunities to change the hearts and minds of the British public on specific issues, but rather a coherent alternative world view. The government and the industry were very aware of the extent to which this view could function as part of a marketing campaign for other goods and services, and for most this was synonymous with the 'American way of life'. For more specific informational and publicity activities, it does seem as if the government was increasingly reliant upon non-theatrical informational materials, and upon indirect subsidy schemes like the Informational Media Guaranty Program.

Notes

1. International Information Division of the State Department, departmental circular, 22 February, 1944, file no 800.4061 - Motion Pictures 409.A.
2. *Morning Post*, July 1958.
3. A. J. P. Taylor, *The Second World War: An Illustrated History* (Putnam, New York, 1964) p. 86.
4. D. Childs, *Britain Since 1945: A Political History* (St Martin's Press, London, 1983) p. 23.
5. *Daily Mail*, 8 October, 1947, cited in F. Vanderschmidt, *What the English Think of Us* (McBride, New York, 1948).

6. S. Horler, *World's Press News*, 22 January 1948.
7. For a recent survey of U S postwar foreign policy, see Charles L. Mee, Jun., *The Marshall Plan; The Launching of the Pax Americana* (Simon and Schuster, New York, 1984).
8. P. Addison, *Now the War is Over; A Social History of Britain, 1945 - 51*, (Jonathan Cape, London, 1985), p. 2.
9. H. M. Pelling, *The Labour Governments, 1945 - 1951* (Macmillan, London, 1984), p. 31.
10. G. Orwell, 'As I Please', *Herald Tribune*, 3 December 1943, reprinted in *Collected Essays, Journalism and Letters of George Orwell, Volume 3: As I Please* (Penguin, London, 1970).
11. T. Harrisson, 'British Opinion Moves Towards a New Synthesis', *Public Opinion Quarterly*, vol. 2, no. 3 (1947), pp. 327-41.
12. British Embassy in Washington D.C., 16 March 1946, cited in Pelling, *Labour Governments*, p. 59.
13. A. Visson, *As Others See Us* (Doubleday, Garden City, New Jersey, 1948), p. 68.
14. V. Cowles, *No Cause For Alarm* (Harper, New York, 1949), p. 316.
15. F Vanderschmidt, *What the English Think of Us*, p. 88.
16. Visson, *As Others See Us*, p. 46.
17. E. Johnston, 'Steady Growth in World Markets', 1955 Annual Report, Motion Picture Export Association.
18. *New York Times*, 1 July, 1937.
19. *Review of Foreign Film Markets During 1936*, Bureau of Foreign and Domestic Commerce, Department of Commerce, April 1937.
20. A.W. MacMahon, 'Memorandum on the postwar international information program of the United States', Department of State working paper, 1945.
21. *Variety*, June 6 1945.
22. MPEA 1955 Annual Report.
23. MacMahon, 'Memorandum'.
24. Political and Economic Planning, *The British Film Industry, 1958* (PEP, London, 1958, p. 135.
25. W. Wanger, '120,000 American Ambassadors', *Foreign Affairs*, vol. 18, no. 1 (1939).
26. S. Kracauer, 'National Types as Hollywood Presents Them', *Public Opinion Quarterly*, vol. 13, no. 1, (1949), pp. 553-72.
27. Wanger, '120,000 American Ambassadors'.

US Cultural Policy in Postwar Britain

28. W. Milbourne Neighbors, US Embassy, London, 'Motion Picture Industry in the United Kingdom, 1948', in US Department of Commerce, Office of International Trade, *World Trade in Commodities*, vol. 7, pt. 4, # 13, April 1949.
29. For accounts of Hollywood politics in the 1940s and 1950s see L. Ceplair and S. Englund, *Inquisition in Hollywood: Politics in the Film Community, 1930-1960* (University of California Press, Los Angeles, 1983), G. Kahn, *Hollywood on Trial: The Story of the Ten Who Were Indicted* (Arno Press, New York, 1972, reprint of the 1948 edition).
30. Vanderschmidt, *What the English Think of Us*, p. 135.
31. *World's Press News*, 22 January 1948.
32. MacMahon, 'Memorandum'.
33. R Katz, 'Projecting America Through Films', *Hollywood Quarterly*, vol. 4, no. 3 (1950), pp. 298-308.
34. 'Information Guaranty Program', Hearing before a Subcommittee on Foreign Relations, 85th Congress, 7 October 1957.

Chapter Eight

Britain's Postwar Film Policy

> A general view of the industry still shows the three main
> characteristics which have been apparent in varying degree
> throughout at least half of the industry's development. These
> features are: the power of the large combines; the extent of
> American interests; and an increasing degree of government
> intervention in the affairs of the industry. [1]

> J. Arthur Rank: 'I am doing this work for my God and my
> country.' [2]

Like many other industries in Britain, the extent of state
involvement in the workings of the film industry is surprising for a
country ostensibly committed to free enterprise. The long history of
state interventionism in the workings of the film industry has recently
been ably chronicled by Sarah Street and Margaret Dickinson. [3] They
note that government regulation has always played an important part
in the activities of the industry. This is especially true in the case of
film finance, although it appears that it is the American model of free
enterprise in motion pictures that is aberrant, rather than the British
experience of state funding for film production, since the United States
has essentially been unique in developing a film industry whose affairs
were not tied directly to state funds and policies.

The motives behind the British government's attempts to regulate,
and police the film industry have altered with time. Initially, public
safety issues were paramount, and were the basis for central and local
government provisions to prevent fire hazards and other threats to
public health and welfare. This notion of public welfare historically
has also extended to regulating people's moral standards as well as their
physical safety, and was the basis for early attempts at film censorship
in Great Britain. Local and central government have always tried to
control the experience of the motion picture audience.

A large portion of the national economy moved into the public sector in Britain during and after the Second World War and the film industry was very much a part of this shift. In the same period, central planning and government control of production were also extended into cultural activities. During the war, for example, institutions like the Council for the Encouragement of Music and the Arts (later, the Arts Council) increasingly brought many types of cultural endeavour into the public domain. The postwar British government's 'film policy' was one of a number of areas where economic and cultural policies met. What is perhaps surprising is that, in the decade after the Second World War, there were few major differences in the ways in which the Labour and the Conservative governments approached the question of film policy. Both were very dubious about the capabilities and integrity of the film industry's financiers, and both initially believed that in many respects the film industry was in a unique financial situation. As a memorandum written in the planning stages of the National Film Finance Corporation put it:

> The film industry is not one which normal financial channels look upon with favour. Its habits are peculiar, most of the people engaged in it are rogues of one kind or another, and a good deal of money has been lost by unwise investment in it, or by the uncontrolled behaviour of producers. The problem therefore seems to be to find an existing organisation (if there is one) or if not, to set up a new one which can venture into this new field with sufficient authority and determination to enable them to make a success of it. [4]

In the postwar decade, motion pictures often figured prominently as a subject for public debate and controversy. Members of Parliament vied with each other to demonstrate their familiarity with the medium and its vocabulary. Almost always, economic affairs ranked near the top of politicians' concerns, although class and intellectual prejudices against the American feature film were rarely absent from their comments: 'Hollywood's good gifts to us in the shape of Walt Disney and the Marx Brothers are few compared with the long list of films which act as a social narcotic and which have merely a brassy vulgarity.' [5]

In the 1930s, the government staunchly maintained that the domestic industry should to be encouraged to challenge Hollywood.

Initially, this took the form of attempting to regulate film distribution and exhibition, with preferential treatment for British films, based on the argument that, without control over exhibition outlets, American producers could not guarantee that they would be able to maintain their share of the market. Very often, concern over the inadequacy of film representation of the British Empire lay at the centre of these early attempts to regulate American films. British audiences saw films about the British Empire, or with the Empire as their backdrop, through American eyes. Similarly, Britain's colonies and dominions saw much more of the United States at the cinema than they saw of Britain. Both were situations which Britain's leaders sought to remedy. At successive Imperial Conferences, representatives acknowledged that film was important as a political and economic tool, and that something had to be done to challenge the United States' supremacy in the field, which threatened to undermine Britain's own imperial authority. Furthermore, the loss of overseas markets outside the Empire, in South America and elsewhere, was explicitly tied to the predominance there of the American feature film. A sub-committee on films at the 1926 Imperial Conference had concluded:

> The importance and far-reaching influence of the cinema are
> now generally recognised. The cinema is not merely a form of
> entertainment but, in addition, a powerful instrument of
> education in the widest sense of that term, and, even where it
> is not used avowedly for purposes of instruction, advertisement
> or propaganda, it exercises indirectly great influence in shaping
> the ideas of the very large numbers to whom it appeals. [6]

The political and intellectual elites in Britain were also worried about their quasi-colonial rule over the rest of the British population within Britain, which, with the emergence of universal suffrage, was one of the major motives behind the emergence of official public relations programmes in the 1930s.

Quotas were used to nurture a domestic industry behind tariff barriers and the government itself embarked upon film production on a very limited scale. This was roughly the situation during the Second World War, when domestic producers profited from restrictions on imports of American feature films - which the war was able to enforce in a way that the British authorities never could. After the war, economic considerations ranked very high on everybody's lists of priorities. Essentially, the postwar Britain economy could not afford American motion pictures in the quantities in which the British people wanted to consume them.

There was also a host of non-economic considerations which shaped British and American actions. Britain was used to having most art forms and the mass media, particularly the press, controlled by just a handful of powerful oligarchs. The feature film was different in that this group did not control it, neither in a commercial nor in an ideological sense. Instead, motion pictures were controlled by another group of powerful men in the United States, and there were frequent attempts to wrest this control away from them. For their part, as Michael Korda notes, the American movie companies 'generally considered themselves to be sovereign states at least equal to the United Kingdom in power'. [7] In many respects, this was borne out in the dealings between the British government and the studios, where negotiations seemed to take the form of meetings between heads of state.

There was a great interest in using the film as a form of internal cultural projection and overseas publicity married to an acute belief in the unique persuasive properties of the new medium. Britain's political elite, both its civil service and its politicians, were acutely conscious of the ideological implications of the external influence over British cinema audiences. For forty years, the British government was actively involved in the development of a 'British film', a term which at times seemed almost to be an oxymoron. The film industry was equally interested in developing a British film, although producers rather than distributors and exhibitors were the ones who wanted to encourage British production. British exhibitors had traditionally placed box office receipts before patriotism.

Amongst producers in Britain however, the campaign for the British film has often appeared selflessly romantic and idealistic. Back in 1922 for example, William Friese-Greene, the father of British cinematography, had collapsed from malnutrition and subsequently died whilst addressing a group of British producers at the Connaught Hotel. He had been speaking about the threat posed by American domination of the film industry. In a similar spirit, twenty-five years later, J. Arthur Rank wagered and lost much of his personal fortune challenging Hollywood in the American market. Rank's father, the biggest flour miller in Britain, had spent much of his life attempting

to set up protectionist tariff barriers to keep American flour out of
Britain. Rank himself wanted to do the same thing with American
films. British producers have always faced the same range of
difficulties in competing with Americans in the British market.
Perhaps their biggest problem has been that, regardless of the actual
content and artistic merit of their films, they could not compete in
terms of budgets with most American films.

The size of the British market has often been blamed for the
inability of British producers to produce more than a handful of high
budget films each year, whereas the spectacle and glamour of lavish
budgets and expensive settings were traditionally a central part of the
appeal of the American film. Consequently, producers have always felt
justified in their demands for protection and some form of subsidy for
production. In most important respects this is still very much the case
today. Thomas Guback, for example, is very pessimistic about the
ability of European countries to develop national cinemas which do
not mimic the American model, partly because of the strength of the
American model, but also as a result of American investment in
European production. [8] The United States remains able to populate
the world's cinema and television screens because it is able to offer
very inexpensive programming for far less than other countries can
produce it. For example, British television currently pays $60,000 for
each new episode of Dallas it shows, and a single segment of this
show costs in excess of $1,000,000 to produce. [9]

Market considerations do not provide a full explanation, however,
because other countries with smaller markets, such as France, were
able to create national traditions of film making and television
programming which were able to compete successfully with the
American product in their own national markets.

In the 1930s, the quota system produced a very artificial situation in
which British film production proliferated and money for independent
producers was very forthcoming. By 1937, Britain was second only to
Hollywood in the number of feature films produced each year.
However, that was also the year when the whole structure of the
British film industry collapsed and it earned a reputation for unstable
finances from which it never recovered. [10] Subsequently, producers
looked to either the Rank Organization or the British government for
support. Essentially, all film producers in Britain found it difficult to
obtain financing, even for very modest productions, and it was

primarily in the area of modest production that the British government chose to invest its efforts.

During the war and immediately afterwards, a number of working parties examined the problems of the availability of production facilities, working capital and the monopoly power exerted by just two major companies, Rank and Associated British Picture Corporation. [11] The British government seriously considered proposals for some form of direct participation in the film industry, which would in most respects be only an extension of the production and exhibition policies pursued during the war. The Film Production Council, for example, which met on a regular basis to discuss the problems of the industry, was an attempt to bring together representatives of different branches of the industry to encourage and to regulate production, just as production councils had regulated the activities of many industries during the war. Some of these government proposals to encourage independent production presupposed that the problem lay in film exhibition and distribution, since the two major companies had very little incentive to encourage or deal with independent producers. A 'third circuit', in which government-run cinemas would compete with the distribution and exhibition monopoly of the Rank and Associated British Picture Corporation, was seriously considered, on the assumption that such a system, which would give independent producers an opportunity to exhibit their films, could be run on the lines of the British Broadcasting Corporation. The Palache Committee, for example, recommended a scheme of production subsidies incoporated into a state-run renting organization. The proposal which was felt to offer the best chance of dealing with American competition, however, was for some form of film bank operated by the state, which would finance independent film productions, and ultimately this was the proposal which carried the day.

The postwar Labour government had many members who were familiar with the workings of the film industry. The most important of these was Sir Stafford Cripps, who before the war had been the legal counsel for the Westminster Bank which had brought suit against some 35 insurance companies who had been less than cautious in financing the film industry's boom period. He was therefore very familiar with the shaky finances and failed optimism of the pre-war British film industry, and this must have shaped his attitude in his dealings with the film industry. Two other younger but important members of the Labour government were also involved in the workings of the industry. Hugh Gaitskell, for example, had been the principal assistant secretary at Board of Trade during the war, and the film industry was a major part of his brief there. He so impressed Rank with his negotiation skills that after the war, when he entered the Commons, Rank and Korda invited him to become vice president and economic advisor of the British Film Producers Association. He acted briefly in this capacity, before other commitments pressured him into resigning, but even when he joined the government in late 1945 he continued to be an honorary vice president of the Association. Finally, there was Harold Wilson, who had no experience of working with the film industry prior to his appointment as President of the Board of Trade, but soon proved there that he had a special interest in the area. He became widely respected within the film trade, especially during the American film embargo, from which he emerged as the hero of the hour, and after leaving the government in 1951 he maintained his interest, including work as a reviewer for a number of books about the film industry. [12]

In April 1948, in the wake of the Anglo-American Film Agreement, which was immediately followed by a decision to establish a 45% quota, a measure as surprising to the Americans as the *ad valorem* tax itself, President of the Board of Trade Harold Wilson announced to the House of Commons he was studying the question of 'affording improved access to finance to qualified independent producers'. Fourteen weeks later he announced plans for the creation of a Film Finance Company, with powers to borrow £2.5 million from its bankers on Treasury guarantee. The Company was replaced in March 1949 by the National Film Finance Corporation set up under the Cinematograph Film Production (Special Loans) Act, 1949, with power to borrow up to £5,000,000 from the Board of Trade. The Corporation's brief was to lend to film distributors, who would in turn make that money available to film producers. Wilson had argued that this special financing was 'required to meet the difficulties of postwar transition'. In other words, the government believed that the film industry's difficulties were purely temporary, and it was hoped that the Film Finance Corporation would be able to put itself out of business in five years or less. [13] Many people opposed lending money to Rank and Korda on the grounds that this would be merely 'refinancing failure', yet there was also a widespread awareness that these two producers had in some ways taken the biggest risks on behalf of the film industry. This posed a real quandary for the government, which gave Brendan Bracken and other members of the opposition many opportunities to poke fun at the expense of the government:

> The government was reluctant to base its rescue operation on individual merit, since it would then be in the position of a film critic, trying to decide which film, producer or director deserved financing with public money. Brendan gave a tongue-in-cheek portrayal of the future, in which the Prime Minister and the members of the cabinet spent their spare time reading film scripts and auditioning actresses and predicted that there would soon be casting couches in Whitehall, and that the Attlee government would finance a musical based on the life of Keir Hardy, or a romantic epic about Sidney and Beatrice Webb. [14]

A shadow board of directors for the Film Finance Company was appointed in September, headed by J. H. Lawrie, an accountant, who left the Industrial and Commercial Finance Corporation to assume this new position. When the National Film Finance Corporation was formally established six months later, appropriately Lord Reith was named as its first chairman, and Lawrie remained with the Corporation as managing director. Reith was never very active in the Corporation - he was once described as being 'strangely silent' in this capacity, and was soon succeeded by Robert Stopford. The real power at the Corporation was Lawrie, who was discovered to have 'an unusual talent not only on the financial side but also on the creative side of the film industry'. [15] The first major borrower was not the Rank Organization but a film distribution company owned by Sir Alexander Korda, the British Lion Film Corporation. British Lion implied that it would be channeling any funds it received from the NFFC to a number of independent producers. British Lion, in fact, became the major client for NFFC funds. The company was controlled by Korda and lent the bulk of its funds to London Films, Korda's major film production company.

Meanwhile, as the decade came to a close, it became increasingly apparent that the Rank Group would not be able to challenge the American film industry after all. Its policy of elaborate productions, aimed at the international market, and a production programme intended to fulfil all the quota needs of its associated cinemas had failed. In November 1949, Rank's Odeon Group reported a huge operating loss of £3,528,615. As *The Economist* suggested, 'The Odeon group, then, is stripped and bare. It has emerged from a disastrous year only by pulling out reserves and bringing in special credits on the grand scale. It will not be able to repeat these devices in a second year .' Rank's losses led *The Economist* to conclude that the difficulties in obtaining financing within the film industry were not a temporary state of affairs and were likely to continue in the long run. This rendered problematic any notion that once the NFFC had 'primed the pump. . . British films can be produced in growing volume on a basis of financial independence'. [16]

In 1950, the bankruptcy of the notion that the NFFC and the British taxpayer would between them be able to fund independent production on a substantial scale was revealed by the creation of the British Film Production Fund. This was a voluntary contribution scheme whereby British exhibitors agreed to subsidize British production out of a levy on cinema admissions. The Eady Levy, as this measure came to be known, raised prices of seats over 1s 6d by a penny and gave producers an extra £1.5 million. In a sense, the British Film Production Fund was the type of association between exhibitors and distributors which ought to have emerged 25 years earlier. Film exhibition had always been profitable in Britain, and this was the first scheme which directly channelled exhibitors' receipts to film producers.

The NFFC grew to be very important indeed for British producers and its loans, although often criticized as 'merely subsidization in disguise', became very important to the film industry. [17] In the first eight and a half years of its operation until March 1957, the Corporation made loans for part of the production costs of 374 long films and 81 shorts, worth a total of £15.7 million. Between 1950 and 1956, 56% of the British first features released on the three main circuits were partially funded with NFFC money. [18] Furthermore, the NFFC was not the massive burden on the taxpayer which its critics claimed. It is true that in its first two years it incurred substantial debts, particularly because of the loan to British Lion, but thereafter its performance improved quickly. The Corporation lost £669,345 in 1949/50, but its loss was only £45,851 in 1952/53, and in 1951/52 it actually recorded a profit of £10,891. By the end of the financial year in 1953, the Corporation had an accumulated deficiency of only £1,410,155. [19]

The creation of the NFFC led the British government into directly financing feature film production on a major scale. It was soon apparent, however, that NFFC funds were not a total remedy for the British film industry. Many critics also saw a major contradiction in using public funds to support film production, since they believed that it was heavy taxation which was responsible for the producers' dilemma in the first place. As Alan Wood put it in an article in the *News Chronicle* in 1950, in Britain, entertainments tax on cinema tickets was twice as heavy as any other country's, so that out of every 1s 9d admission, some 8.5 pence went to the government as Entertainment Tax. In 1949, when £108,000,000 was taken at the box office, fully £38 million went to the Treasury, whilst producers received only £7.5 millions. He calculated that, even assuming producers received perhaps another £4 million from export sales, this was still £4 million less than their films cost to make. As he succinctly concluded, 'So making films is like taking up heavy-weight boxing. An exceptional film can show a profit but if you go on long enough you are certain to be knocked out in the end.' [20] Other critics, like Nicholas Davenport, a former board member of the National Film Finance Company, maintained that the Corporation was evolving into a virtual dictatorship which was forcing independent producers into the arms of the big concerns, and was much too reliant upon just one company, British Lion. As early as 1951, Davenport was campaigning for the liquidation NFFC. As he put it,

> That the government should have had the courage to wind up the ill-fated groundnuts scheme after an expenditure of £ 36.5 million might encourage the innocent to believe that it will also be bold enough to wind up the NFFC on the spending of its 'gone with the wind' £6 million. [21]

The infiltration of public funds into the British film industry after the war was in many ways the culmination of a process which had begun in the mid-1920s, when official bodies like the Empire Marketing Board had first initiated government film production in peacetime. The EMB briefly had pursued a plan to make a feature film about the British Empire, based upon a treatment by Rudyard Kipling, and directed by Walter Creighton, an individual without any film-making experience, prior to committing itself to an altogether different course, the sponsorship of documentary films. It had taken a quarter of a century for the government to move from this position to direct involvement in feature film production.

Group Three

Sir Wilfred Eady took the responsibility for trying to spend NFFC money on 'new teams', rather than just trying to shore up the finances of the ailing giants in the industry. In May 1950, in a confidential report, he admitted that, although London Films and a small number of other ventures had been saved by the NFFC, 'no new "teams" of promise have emerged and no new pattern of production has shown itself.' He advocated the creation of a film unit 'to get back some of the artistic excitement which was the motive power of the young men who went into the Empire Marketing Board, Crown Film Unit, etc., and to get the same concept of the team spirit which was the remarkable part of that effort'. He wanted to 'break through some of the present gloom and incidentally to see whether we can find a way of maintaining British production without having to subsidise it any further beyond the £6 million in the Film Finance Corporation'. [22] Eady suggested that this new unit ought to be headed by a young aggressive producer, and suggested Harry Watt for the post. Word of the new project got to Grierson, and his response was to write to John Lawrie listing all the possible candidates for the position and their relative attributes, implying all the time that he was the strongest candidate and that he was resigning from his position at the Central Office of Information and so would be available at the end of the year. Writing about the 'group problem which is on all our minds', Grierson noted that he had pioneered both low-budget production in Britain and also large-scale government film production in Canada:

> In this special field, all you have to do is find a man, trust him and back him with both authority and money; for a given period and within a set of terms of reference to be clearly defined from the outset. No committee production, please, and in the name of God! No overhanging other authority, however concealed! This trust and authority established between Tallents and myself was the key to the EMB GPO development. It was likewise between Mackenzie King and myself, with similar results.

I further propose that it be an *independent* set-up, except as it is related to a specific distribution arrangement. Let's have no incidental shadow of Mick (Balcon) and Alex (Korda) over it. If indeed you have picked your man aright, he should be as good as Mick and Alex and, no more than they, likely to take anybody else's masterminding'

The group project appears to have been from the first a redefinition of that approach to production with which I am associated ... I shall in any event be forming a new group next year, as a break from the confining limits of government production under its existing and logical enough terms of reference. To that end I have resigned from the C.O.I. as of the end of the year [23]

Grierson's candidacy for the post of head of a new unit devoted to low-budget and second feature productions found a lot of support. Eady's plan eventually took the form of grouping some independent producers with Rank at Pinewood (Group I), another group to work with Associated British at Elstree (Group II), and Grierson's group of young and new talent, Group III. Like many other Griersonian ideas, it was ahead of its time, and suffered from the decline both of the double bill and also of the total cinema audience.

The Conservative government which came into power in 1951, although hostile to government intervention into the activities of many other industries, found itself in agreement with the Labour government on support for the British film industry. It pursued the same policy of protection, subsidy and support. However, within a short time after the Conservatives came to power, British film producers and exhibitors discovered that their real enemy was not Hollywood, but television. Starting in 1951, cinema admissions in Britain fell precipitately. In 1957, in a very sombre report, Political and Economic Planning found that total cinema admissions were down a full third from total admissions in 1951, and were a full 40% below admissions in 1946. In fact, total admissions in 1957 stood at only 915 million for the whole year. This was actually less than admissions in 1936. It was estimated that every new television license led to the loss of a hundred cinema admissions a year. [24] As John Spraos noted, this was very much a self-perpetuating process. Only half of the declining cinema admissions in Britain could be explained by the growth of television; the rest were, according to his analysis, largely explained by the closure of marginally profitable and unprofitable cinemas which denied many potential cinemagoers any opportunity to continue going to the cinema. [25]

The gradual decline of the British film industry has continued until the present day. This is not to argue, of course, that declining cinema admissions should in any respect be correlated with the artistic qualities of the British film. In fact, once the industry ceased to be so interested in profits or competition with Hollywood, it could be argued that it went on to produce some of its most creative and innovative work. However, there is no question that the British cinema has ceased to be a central social institution in the way that it used to be, or as it remains in most other countries today. Nevertheless, in the 1950s, the British government continued to operate on the assumption that it was important, for national prestige and for a variety of cultural reasons, that it continue to fund the activities of the film industry.

The cultural and public relations aspects of the British government's involvement in the film industry rapidly receded in significance in the course of the fifties, as it became increasingly evident that the motion picture was not the dominant force which it had been a decade earlier. The government might be joined by concerned social organizations in periodically railing against the bad example being set by the American motion picture for its own teenagers, but few people continued to argue that the cinema was functioning as *the* major socializing influence in Britain.

The fall from grace for the cinema in Britain as a major social institution and as the principal vehicle for Americanization in Britain was accompanied by a withdrawal of interest in the government's own film production programme, signalled by the abolition of the Central Office of Information in 1951. After a phase of dramatic expansion during the Second World War, official public relations in Britain fell from favour and this was a fate shared by other official excursions into film production, such as the work of the British documentary movement and the Crown Film Unit. The Labour Party, when for the first time in control of a majority government in Britain, had proven surprisingly inept in its information and public relations policies, and this proved very detrimental to both the extensive official public relations system which had been built, including the Central Office of Information, and most aspects of its official film production programme. [26]

By, say, 1955, the cinema was no longer regarded as being on the cutting edge of Anglo-American relations. The indices of the Parliamentary proceedings, *The Times* and *The Economist* a decade earlier had been filled with references to the discussion of the fate of 'the British Film', and the threat of Americanization. These now no longer seemed to be such pressing and momentous issues. During the 1950s and 1960s, there continued to be a vast literature on the process of Americanization, but written primarily from the pessimistic view that little could be done to stem the appeal of American popular culture in Europe.

On one level, the decision to de-emphasize state action directed against the American feature film was simple expediency. The film industry had been swept along by the tide of nationalization under the Labour governments. On their return to power, the Conservatives chose to keep state control primarily in those industries, like the railways and the coal industry, where private enterprise would have great difficulty making a profit, but whose continued operation was essential to the industrial infrastructure. It was difficult to argue that there was this kind of direct interdependence between the film industry and other industries. By the mid-1950s, the film industry had begun the commercial decline which has continued down until the present day. If the British cinema audience was increasingly reluctant to see films of any sort, then they were certainly unlikely to pay admission to see the British films to which they had been perennially hostile. Exceptions to this were broadly produced comedy films, such as the Norman Wisdom films in the 1950s, and the whole cycle of 'Carry On' films. Films such as these had the same sort of appeal for provincial audiences which had been responsible for the success of the Formby and Fields films in the 1930s. In other words, modestly produced comedy films could expect to make a profit in Britain in the 1950s, but few other films could.

A decade after the end of the Second World War, the process of Americanization had gone very far - the Britain of the affluent fifties had increasingly taken the United States as its role model for a whole range of commercial and social imperatives. This would provide a great deal of grist for people like Richard Hoggart and Josephine Kleine, who examined the consequences of the commercialization and manufactured nature of British popular culture. Richard Hoggart, for example, noted in his seminal work on changing British working class culture in the 1950s that the 'growing minor mythology imported from America' had had a great impact upon working class culture, especially amongst the young. He also believed that a strain of 'progressivism', new to Britain in the 1950s, and synonymous with shiny material appliances and a rejection of the past and the old-fashioned, was directly related to the effects of Americanization. As he put it:

> The acceptance of 'progressivism', as of much else discussed here, is effected as much by American films as by our own publicists . . . the most striking feature in (British) working class attitudes to America is not a suspicion, though there is often that, nor a resentment at 'bossiness', but a large readiness to accept. This arises mainly from the conviction that in most things the Americans can 'show us a thing or two' about being up to date. In so far as to be up to date is felt to be important, America is the leader; and to be up to date is being made to seem very important. [27]

The British government was incapable of leading a rearguard action against the American feature film. The principal lesson of 25 years of dealing with the film industry seemed to be that only during times of national emergency could government and industry work together, and that only then could the industry be sure of making a profit. By 1955, the debate over Americanization and the mass media had already begun to be diverted to television, and there the same sort of debate which had always surrounded the film industry came to characterize discussions about commercial television. At the time of writing (1985), there are plans to phase out government subsidy for film producers. However, it is significant that this has only been planned after another kind of support, Channel Four, which has been very active in independent production, has come into being.

Notes

1. Political and Economic Planning, *The British Film Industry*, (PEP, London, 1958), quoting the 1952 report, p. 134.
2. A. Wood, *Mr Rank* (Hodder and Stoughton, London, 1953), p. 269.

3. M. Dickinson and S. Street, *Cinema and State, The Film Industry and the British Government, 1927-1984* (British Film Institute, London, 1985).

4. Undated Board of Trade Minute, 'Film Finance', 1948? BT 64/2366.

5. Hansard, 21 January 1948.

6. Appendices, Imperial Conference, 1926, Report of the General Sub-Committee on Films, CMD 2769, p. 403.

7. M. Korda, *Charmed Lives; A Family Romance* (Random House, New York, 1979), p. 219.

8. T. Guback, ''Cultural Identity and Film in the European Economic Community', *Cinema Journal,* vol. 14, no. 1 (1974), pp. 2 - 15.

9. *Fortune*, 5 September, 1985

10. S. Legg and F. D. Klingender, *Money Behind the Screen* (Film Centre, London, 1937).

11. The Gater Committee was constituted in July 1948 to examine the studio space shortage and whether the government should own its own studio space; it reported in November of the same year; the Plant Committee on film distribution and exhibition also reported in 1948. In addition, the Film Production Council, of which the President of the Board of Trade was the chair, reported regularly on the affairs of the British film industry.

12. H. Wilson, Review of 1952 PEP. report on the British Film Industry, *Sight and Sound*, July (1951).

13. 'Film Finance', *The Economist*, 21 July 1948, pp. 191-2.

14. Korda, *Charmed Lives*, p. 220.

15. Brief for Second Reading, Cinematograph Film Production (Special Loans) Bill, 16 November 1953, BT 228/363.

16. 'Films and the Future', *The Economist*, 12 November 1949, pp. 1076-8.

17. N. Davenport, 'The Taxpayer's Stake in Films', *Financial Times*, 18 January, 1951.

18. PEP, *The British Film Industry*, 1958, p. 133.

19. Brief for Second Reading.

20. A. Wood, 'Why Our Films Lose Money', *News Chronicle*, 9 December, 1950.

21. Davenport 'Taxpayer's Stake in Films'.

22. Eady to Trend, 31 May 1950, T228/273.

23. Grierson to Lawrie, 1 October 1950 T228/273.

24. PEP, *The British Film Industry*, 136.
25. J. Spraos, *The Decline of the Cinema: An Economist's Report* (Allen and Unwin, London, 1962), pp. 20-2.
26. A. A. Rogow, 'The Public Relations Program of the Labor Government and British Industry', *Public Opinion Quarterly*, vol. 16, no. 2 (1952).
27. R. Hoggart, *The Uses of Literacy* (Chatto and Windus, London, 1957), p. 190.

Chapter Nine

Conclusion: Britain and the Consumer Society

> The 'reign of terror' which certain newspapers sought to
> exercise over the cinema industry by turning public sentiment
> against American films seems to have fizzled out, thanks to
> the prompt and vigorous action taken by the trade and its
> press. [1]

During the First World War American motion pictures became the
most conspicuous example of the globalization of American popular
culture. The United States is as secure today in this cultural dominion
as it has ever been. Fewer people watch American films in Britain
than used to be the case in the 1930s and 1940s, but this is primarily
because far fewer people go to the cinema than they did thirty years
ago. If British television audiences today watch a much lower
percentage of American programming on their television sets than
their parents and grandparents did on their cinema screens, this is
largely because the government is able to regulate American television
programming to a much greater extent than it was ever able to regulate
American films. For fifty years, successive governments attempted to
control the proportion of American films shown on British screens,
but never with the success with which a 15% limit is currently
imposed upon the amount of British prime time television
programmes originating outside the Common Market. A recent report
of the European Parlement affirmed that the United States currently
holds 70% of the film market in Greece, 80% in the Netherlands, and a
massive 92% in Britain. The only exception to the US domination of
European screens in fact, is France, which has managed to retain
almost 50% of its domestic market, and which has actually had a
marked success in penetrating the American market. [2] In general,
American motion pictures and television programming have been very
successful in capturing the European markets, continuing the policies
chronicled throughout this book. American product accounts for

one out of every two films shown in Europe, and two out of every three television programmes.

Films are a very different order of information flow from telecommunications. Broadcasting is, by its very definition, ubiquitous, and new technological developments constantly act to make it increasingly so. Motion pictures in one sense have a very concrete existence as canisters containing prints of films, which gives them a very material, almost Victorian, commodity status. It is perhaps not surprising, then, that on both sides of the Atlantic civil servants and film producers have traditionally considered motion pictures as commodity form, as signalled, for example, by Acts of Parliament and Board of Trade regulations which discussed motion pictures on the basis of costing so much per foot. The major distinction they have always made between motion pictures and other commodities, however, has been an acute awareness of the power of motion pictures to sell other commodities, whether ideas or much more physical goods and services.

Given the commercial imperatives underlying all aspects of film production, it was very hard to develop an indigenous tradition of film production or a philosophy of film in Britain that was in any way truly national in character - as opposed to colonial and essentially derivative from the American example. Beginning in the years immediately after the First World War, there were repeated demands from the political and cultural establishments in Britain for the self-conscious creation of such a national cinema. The British Film Institute, the National Film Finance Corporation, a large body of government legislation, on-going public debate about the fate of the 'British Film' in the House of Commons and the correspondence pages of *The Times*, and attempts at alternative modes of production like the British documentary movement were all part of this milieu.

The very rarity of successes experienced by film makers in Britain - the British documentary film tradition, the British 'quality' film, social realism, and the revival of indigenous production in Britain in the last decade - has made the accomplishments of British cinema all the more spectacular and significant. British film historians have always been eager to identify an innately British tradition of film, since conspicuous British achievements in virtually every other cultural domain have tended to highlight the relative sparsity of Britain's prowess in film.

Assessments of the contribution of Britain to the historical development of film as form have often stressed the continuity between the work of successive generations of British film makers. Tied to this idea of continuity in British film is the notion that realism and the actuality-based film are in some way an essentially British contribution to film theory and practice. This interpretation seeks to place the whole utilitarian Griersonian documentary tradition, social realism in its various forms, and bodies of filmmaking as disparate as the early primitivism of the Brighton School and Ealing Studios into the same tradition. In a sense, such an argument erects a model of British cinema as consistently in opposition to the dominant Hollywood model.

Hollywood's principal assets were 'glamour', 'vitality', material surplus, and a whole range of values tied to the 'high quality' which the Washington Chamber of Commerce was conscious were the main attractions of American feature films and stars to overseas audiences. The twin ideologies of glamour and consumerism were retailed overseas in Hollywood's films, and also in all the paraphernalia of film promotion and sales: the star system, the publicity and press material, the advertising campaigns, the pin-ups and the personal appearances. For five years after the war, the British film industry made a concerted effort to replicate the style and sentiment of the Hollywood film. The Rank Organization, the only British studio ever to rival the size and the ambitions of the Hollywood majors, attempted initially to mimic their budgets, their production techniques and their star system. Yet, as we have seen, Hollywood's production values and sensibilities consistently eluded Rank. The only 'high quality' films made in Britain during this period which were successful tended to be the handful of expensive epics produced each year: film adaptations of Dickens and Shakespeare or other types of excursion into the classical arts, like *The Red Shoes*. It would be reasonable to argue that generally expensive British productions failed when they tried to imitate Hollywood's techniques too faithfully, such as the big budgets and stars of *Caesar and Cleopatra* and the style of the Hollywood musical in *London Town*.

American feature films projected a coherent world view which crossed lines of authorship, genre and even the production contexts of specific studios. This view was rooted in optimism, expansiveness and growth, all qualities which had been synonymous with 'the American way of life' for over fifty years. In some respects, it was these self-same qualities which had been at the centre of the debate over 'Americanization' in fields as diverse as the arts, industry and commerce since the beginning of the century. In the United States, there was a widespread awareness that it was these qualities which made their films, as well as their other cultural forms so appealing to overseas audiences. This, for example, led the American cultural attache in London to conclude whilst comparing British and American film production techniques:

> It is very difficult to draw a comparison between the production techniques of United States films and that of the British. In general, British films tend to be of the quiet, narrative type, with historical pictures predominating. The production technique exhibited in films of this type has been very successful. The United States films, which are fast moving, and with a strong dramatic or entertainment technique have their own appeal in the United Kingdom. [3]

Even in the late 1940s, there was a recognition that British and American films provided the cinema audience with different orders of experience. It is equally evident, however, that the major British conglomerate was for a time locked into the strategy of trying to copy the American film. For a brief period, the British government agreed that the film industry had adopted an appropriate position. The official reports on the availability of studio space, for example, were based on the assumption that if the facilities were available, British filmmakers could make films that would successfully separate Hollywood from its British audiences. However, it was actually modesty - a quality almost antithetical to Hollywood's dominant aesthetic - which characterized those British films which were commercially successful in the postwar decade.

Films like the Ealing comedies, the pre-war output of the Griersonian school, Group Three, the British free cinema movement and the 'kitchen sink drama' style of social realism in the 1960s can be bound together. Perhaps the thing which binds them most strongly is their rejection, in varying degrees, of the Hollywood aesthetic. None of these British film-making traditions attempt to provide the cinema audience with the same experience as the typical Hollywood film. In hindsight, the decisions to aim for modest production values, a location, not a studio, aesthetic, and subject matter grounded in the realities of life in postwar Britain can all be viewed as an overt and deliberate rejection of Hollywood. In some instances, like Griersonian documentary, there was a very conscious philosophical rejection of what Hollywood sold. For John Grierson, Hollywood was merely 'showmanship built on garish spectacle and a red hot presentation of the latest curves'. [4] For others, like Ealing Studios, sophisticated management techniques coupled with a studio style not rooted in sound stage production led to an equally non-Hollywood approach. The decision to defy comparisons with Hollywood even made it possible for the Ealing films to appeal to the American audience, as well as the British audience.

On one level, the commercial and critical successes of some of those British films which steered away from Hollywood in terms of production values were the result of a wise strategy. In postwar Britain it was very difficult indeed for an expensive British film to cover production costs in the home market. In 1949, for example, Associated British Picture released *My Brother Jonathan*, which was a relatively successful film at the British box office, obtaining a final total take of £1,020,000. Of this total, Entertainments Tax took £416,000, exhibitors took £375,000, the renter received £57,000 and the producer £192,000. Since the film cost £198,000 to produce, the producer actually lost money on a box office hit. [5] Consequently, there was a lot of interest in streamlining production methods, such as the 'independent frame' technique, in cutting costs, and, in general, in attempting to make expensive films cheaply!

It is easier to document the experiences of the film viewer and of film exhibition in Britain than the work of indigenous film-makers, although the temptation to fixate upon the work of the filmmaker rather than the film consumer remains strong. American films provided British audiences with experiences which they could not get from either British films or most other cultural forms. During the postwar decade, their importance to the British people did change. In 1945, cinema stood alone as the only available unrationed luxury. A decade later, commercial television, changing audience demographics and changing leisure patterns had reduced the numbers of people who regularly saw American films. After the war, there were regular discussions about the impact of American films on working people, most of whom went to the cinema at least once a week. A decade later, most of the critical concern about film revolved around the impact of cinema upon the young, who were increasingly the major constituency for the film industry. Nevertheless, although American feature films were perhaps less pervasive as a social institution after the war, they continued to be the most widespread means of disseminating American popular culture overseas. In the early fifties, people in Britain still spent twice as much at the cinema as 'they spent on going to theatres, concert-halls, music halls, dance halls, skating rinks, sporting events and all other places of popular entertainment'. [6] This did not last, because the advent of commercial television eroded cinema admissions very rapidly. There were 4,500,000 television licenses in March 1955, and this figure had risen to 8,000,000 less than three years later. The initial television set owners tended to be relatively wealthy and not particularly avid cinemagoers. However, starting in 1955, when prices for television sets began to go down and commercial television broadcasting began in Britain, television did successfully wean viewers away from the cinema. From this point on, as John Spraos put it, 'each new (television) set dealt a heavy blow to the cinema'. [7]

Social and cultural commentators remained critical of the 'bread and circuses' mentality which they felt pervaded American feature films. Josephine Klein, talked about the film preferences of the people of Ashton in the mid-1950s:

> The films that are seen resemble one another in their irrele-
> vance to the problems of the day. When Ashton people visit the
> cinema, they protect themselves by attending only those films
> which portray events so utterly remote from any they know that
> their portrayal has no real impact on their lives. [8]

Films, like other types of American popular culture had, to quote Wim Wenders, succeeded in colonizing Europe's imagination. In postwar Britain, American images had a decided impact upon British imaginations. As part of the social history of the postwar decade, it is clear that Britain was a principal beneficiary - or victim - of Americanization. Sometimes this was a consequence of conscious cultural policy, on the part of the culture industries and the American government. More generally it was linked to the commercial basis and commercializing nature of American cultural forms as a whole. This gave these forms a dynamic appeal which made them very attractive to

European audiences, who were especially vulnerable to outside influences in the postwar years. Also, and this was very apparent to the European intelligentsia, American popular culture was often more attractive and appealing to the working classes of Britain and elsewhere than anything they themselves could produce.

At the beginning of this century social and cultural critics had first documented the 'Americanisation' of their own people. Fifty years later, they saw the signs and symptoms of American popular culture everywhere, and saw little competing with it. Hollywood's lessons in consumption were an important part of the way of educating the people of Britain and most other countries after the war. The American motion picture's vision of an open, mobile, materially endowed culture was very attractive to any country which was just beginning to acquire these things. Many European commentators believed that the U S A had been markedly more successful in exporting overseas a taste for its merchandise than in retailing its ideas and politics. Robert Jungk, writing on Americanisation and technocracy argued that:

> 'One of the characteristics of the American revolution appears
> to be its inability, when brought into contact with foreign
> cultures, to compel intellectual and spiritual acceptance of its
> own politico-spiritual principles . . . It is not America's
> political ideas but, in most cases, its goods which are accepted
> by other people and have a revolutionary effect. American
> goods - powerful bulldozers, cigarettes, small cheap amateur
> cameras and giant transformers - have, during the past fifteen
> years or so, spread all over the world, acting as missionaries for
> the American way of life' [9]

It would be simplistic to suggest that American popular cultural forms provided Britain with a blueprint for the type of society which evolved there in the years after the war. Although there are many who would argue otherwise, Britain has not become a colonial outpost of the United States, at least in a cultural sense. Nevertheless, like many other aspects of American popular culture, motion pictures were appropriated in virtually all of Europe, and perhaps nowhere is this more true than in Great Britain. The 'new materialism' of Britain in the fifties was often linked to the lessons taught by American culture, as were many of the other changes accompanying the return to peace and the retreat from a planned, centralised economy and society and towards a more free enterprise model. By the mid-1950s, Britain was scarcely recognizable as the country which had been suffering from the effects of the war, exhaustion and bankruptcy a decade earlier. This was true in a social sense too. People demanded new social relations as well as new material possessions during the course of the 1950s. Thirty years later, it appears as if Britain has been quite successful in obtaining material goods on American lines, but rather less so in replicating the American class system. It has become common to maintain that Britain has not done as well as many of its neighbours in developing a consumer culture on American lines. As Tom Hooson put it recently, Britain seems prepared to accept a lower material standard of living than many Western European countries as the trade-off for greater leisure time. Yet at the same time, there is still a widespread interest in developing a consumer society in Britain:

> American ideas are so fundamental to consumer society that it is arguable that the national genius of the Americans was necessary for originating the modern consumer society. It is the product of the same principles on which the American nation itself is founded . . . The fruits of prosperity are highly acceptable, but it is not always clear whether America's imitators wish to accept the price to be paid for them. England exhibits more schizophrenia than most contemporary states. Englishmen are now whole-hearted consumers, but they have a half-hearted appetite for working hard enough to expand the system that provides their livelihood. [10]

The process of Americanization has gone a very long way, and the view of most commentators on media imperialism would seem to be that American hegemony in Europe is as complete as it has ever been.[11] Nevertheless, it ought perhaps to be remembered that for three decades, the debate over Americanization in Britain often revolved quite specifically around the issue of American motion pictures. This same debate continues to the present day, the only major difference being that American television is the main culprit. Today, Anglo-American cultural policies are in most respects no more sophisticated than they were thirty years ago, what has changed primarily are the technologies and media distribution systems. Its also appears that the British film industry is still playing very much the same game it played forty years ago.

At the time of writing, the *Wall Street Journal* reported on the state of the British film industry in the wake of 1985's 'British Film Year'. Britain's exhibitors are in dire straits, with an estimated weekly clientele of only 1.5 million - about 5% of their audience forty years ago. Of course, home use of video casette recorders has exacerbated the plight of the British film industry. Britain has the world's highest per capita ownership of video machines and consumption of motion pictures remains high, however, this has been of only very limited benefit to domestic film producers. Britain's only remaining major film producer, Goldcrest, appears to be in severe financial difficulties, brought on specifically by recent failures of expensive films such as Revolution aimed quite primarily at the American market. Goldcrest's management maintain that they must get at least 70% of the return on their films from the American market, or they will not make a profit.[12] Goldcrest's recent problems seem very reminscent of the experiences of Rank in the postwar decade, and raise doubts about the prospects of Britain ever surmounting the problems of American domination of the British film market place.

In the meantime, when often the most avid topic of discussion between two British people may well be what happened on this week's episode of *Dallas* or *Dynasty*, it is clear that the process of usurping British popular culture begun at the beginning of this century has gone as far as those selling American media abroad had hoped, and much further than those who tried to prevent this very thing from happening had feared.

Notes

1. *The Cinema*, 2 March 1916, from Golden Jubilee of KRS programme, 1956.
2. 'When it Comes to Movies, the World Looks to America', *New York Times*, 22 September 1985.
3. W. Milbourne Neighbors, U.S. Embassy, 'Motion Picture Industry in the United Kingdom, 1948, in Department Of Commerce, Office Of International Trade, *World Trade In Commodities*, vol. 7, pt. 4, # 13, April 1949

4. J. Grierson, 'The Course of Realism', C. Davy (ed.), *Footnotes to the Film* (Lovat Dickson, London, 1937), p. 203.
5. 'Finance For Films', *The Economist*, 11 December 1948.
6. Political and Economic Planning, *The British Film Industry* (PEP, London, 1952), p. 17.
7. J. Spraos, *The Economic Decline of the Cinema: An Economist's Report* (Allen and Unwin, London, 1962), p. 22.
8. J. Klein, *Samples from English Culture*, (Routledge and Kegan Paul, London, 1965), p. 91.
9. R. Jungk, 'Europe and American Technocracy', in UNESCO, *The Old and the New World* (UNESCO, New York, 1956), p. 222.
10. T. Hooson, 'Exporting the Pursuit of Happiness, in R Rose (ed.), *Lessons from America : An Exploration*(John Wiley, New York,1974), p. 162.
11. The domination of European television markets by American exports is discussed at length in T Gitlin, *Inside Prime Time* (Pantheon, New York, 1985).
12. *'British Movies Aren't Better Than Ever, But, Then, What Is'*, *Wall Street Journal*, 4 March, 1986.

Select Bibliography

Primary Sources

UK Board of Trade documents
UK Treasury documents
US Department of Commerce documents

Printed Primary Sources

Bernstein Questionaire, (Granada, London, 1947)
'Informational Media Guaranty Program', Hearing before a
  Subcommittee of the Committee on Foreign Relations, United
  States Senate, 85th Congress, 7 October 1957
MacMahon, A.W. *'Memorandum on the Postwar International
  Information Program of the United States'*, Department of State
  working paper, 1945
Moss, L. and Box, K. *The Cinema Audience: An Enquiry made by the
  Wartime Social Survey for the Ministry of Information* (Ministry of
  Information, London, 1943)
Motion Picture Association of America, *Annual Reports*
  _____*'Delinquent Children . . . A World Problem'* (Motion Picture
  Export Association, London, 1950)
Motion Picture Division, Bureau of Foreign and Domestic Commerce,
  US Department of Commerce. *Review of Foreign Film Markets*
  March 1939
Motion Picture Export Association. Annual Reports
Report of the Departmental Committee on Chidren and the Cinema
  (HMSO, London, 1950)

Screen Advertising Association. *The Cinema Audience: A National Survey* (Screen Advertising Association, London, 1961)

Books

Abrams, M. *The Teenage Consumer* (London Press Exchange, London, 1959)

Addison, P. *Now the War is Over : A Social History of Britain, 1945-51* (Jonathan Cape, London, 1985)

Aldgate, A. and Richards, J. *The Best of British: Cinema and Society, 1930-1970* (Blackwell, London, 1983)

Armes, R. *A Critical History Of British Cinema* (Oxford University Press, London, 1978)

Austin, B. (ed.), *Current Research in Film, Vol I : Audiences, Economics and Law* (Ablex, New Jersey, 1985)

Balcon, M. *Michael Balcon Presents . . . A Lifetime of Films* (Hutchinson, London, 1969)

Barr, C. *Ealing Studios* (Cameron and Tayleur, London, 1977)

Barrett, M. *et al. Ideology And Cultural Production* (Croom Helm, London, 1979)

Benjamin, W. *Illuminations* (Schocken, New York, 1969)

Bigsby, C.W. E. *Superculture: American Popular Culture and Europe* (Elek, London, 1975)

Biskind, P. *Seeing is Believing; How Hollywood Taught Us to Stop Worrying and Love the Fifties* (Pantheon, New York, 1983)

Bogarde, D. *Snakes and Ladders* (Chatto and Windus, London, 1978)

Box, K. *The Cinema and the Public* (Central Office of Information, London, 1947)

Brady, R. A. *Crisis in Britain* (Cambridge University Press, London, 1950)

Brantlinger, P. *Bread and Circuses: Theories of Mass Culture as Social Decay* (Cornell University Press, Ithaca, New York, 1983)

Brode, D. *The Films of the Fifties:* Sunset Blvd *to* On The Beach (Citadel Press, Secaucus, 1976)

Brogan, D.W. *American Themes* (Hamish Hamilton, London, 1948)

Burnham, J. (ed.) *What Europe Thinks of America* (John Day, New York, 1953)

Calvocoressi, P. *The British Experience, 1945-1975* (Pantheon, London, 1978)

Carter, P. A. *Another Part of the Fifties* (Columbia University Press, New York, 1983)

Clarke, R. *Anglo-American Economic Collaboration in War and Peace, 1942-1949* (Clarendon Press, Oxford, 1982)

Commager, H. Steele *The American Mind; An Interpretation of American Thought and Character Since the 1880s* (Yale University Press, New Haven, 1950)

_____*Britain Through American Eyes* (McGraw-Hill, New York, 1975)

Cowles, V. *No Cause for Alarm* (Harper, New York, 1949)

Curran, J. and Porter, V. (eds.) *British Cinema History* (Weidenfeld and Nicholson, London, 1983)

Dalton, H. *High Tide and After* (Frederick Muller, London, 1962)

Davies, P. and Neve, B. *Cinema, Politics and Society in America* (University of Manchester Press, Manchester, 1981)

Davy, C. (ed.) *Footnotes to the Film* (Lovat Dickson, London, 1937)

Dickinson, M. and Street, S. *Cinema and State; The Film Industry and the British Government,1927 - 1984* (British Film Institute, London, 1985)

Durgnat, R. *A Mirror for England* (Faber, London, 1970)

Dyer, R. *The Stars* (British Film Institute, London, 1979)

Feuer, J. *The Hollywood Musical* (Indiana University Press, Bloomington, 1982)

Gallup, G. H. (ed.)*The Gallup International Public Opinion Polls, Great Britain, 1937 - 1975* (Random House, New York, 1976)

Gitlin, T. *Inside Prime Time* (Pantheon, New York, 1983)

Gorer, G. *The American People: A Study in National Character* (Norton, New York, 1948)

_____ *Exploring English Character* (Criterion, New York, 1955)

Gow, G. *Hollywood in the Fifties* (Tantivy Press, London, 1971)

Gramsci, A. *Prison Notebooks: Selections* (International Publishers, New York, 1971)

Granger, S. *Sparks Fly Upward* (Granada, London, 1981)

Guback, T. *The International Film Industry: Western Europe and America since 1945* (Indiana University Press, Bloomington, 1969)

Handel, L. A. *Hollywood Looks at its Audience* (University of Illinois Press, Urbana, 1950)

Harley, J. E. *World-wide Influences of the Cinema* (University of Southern California Press, Los Angeles, 1940)

Hebdige, D. *Subculture: The Meaning of Style* (Methuen, London, 1979)

Hewison, R. *In Anger: Culture in the Cold War, 1945-1960* (Weidenfield and Nicolson, London, 1981)

Higham C. and Greenberg, J. *Hollywood in the Forties* (Tantivy Press, London, 1968)

Hoggart, R. *The Uses of Literacy* (Chatto and Windus, London, 1957)

Hopkins, H. *England is Rich: A Portrait at Mid-Century* (Harrap, London, 1957)

_____*The New Look* (Secker and Warburg, London, 1963)

Hudson, M. *Super Imperialism: The Economic Strategy of American Empire* (Holt, Reinhart and Winston, New York, 1971)

Hulton Research, *Patterns of English Life* (Hulton, London, 1948)

Hutton, G. *We Too Can Prosper* (Allen and Unwin for the British Productivity Council, London, 1952)

Jarvie, I. C. *Movies and Society* (Basic Books, New York, 1970)

Johnston, E. *We're All In It* (E. P. Dutton, New York, 1948)

Kallen, H. M. *Culture and Democracy in the United States* (Boni and Liveright, New York, 1924)

Klein, J. *Samples from English Culture* (Routledge and Kegan Paul, London, 1965)

Klingender F. D. and Legg, S. *Money Behind the Screen* (Film Centre, London, 1937)

Korda, M. *Charmed Lives: A Family Romance* (Random House, New York, 1979)

Leavis F. R. and Thompson, D. *Culture and Environment* (Chatto and Windus, London, 1933)

Leavis, Q. D. *Fiction and the Reading Public* (Russell and Russell, London, 1965, 1st edn 1932)

Lowenthal, L. *Literature, Popular Culture and Society* (Prentice-Hall, Englewood Cliffs, 1961)

McCreary, E. A. *The Americanisation of Europe* (Doubleday, New York, 1964)

MacDonald, D. *Against the American Grain* (Gollancz, London, 1963)

Maltby, R. *Harmless Entertainment: Hollywood and the Ideology of Consensus* (Scarecrow Press, Metuchen, NJ, 1983)

Manvell, R. *The Film and the Public* (Penguin, London, 1955)

Marwick, A. *British Society Since 1945* (Allen Lane, London, 1982)

Mass Observation, *Puzzled People* (Gollancz, London, 1947)

Mayer, J. P. *Sociology of the Film* (Faber, London, 1947)

_____ *British Cinemas and Their Audiences* (Dennis Dobson, London, 1948)

Mee, C. L. Jun. *The Marshall Plan: The Launching of the Pax Americana* (Simon and Schuster, New York, 1984)

Morgan, G. *Red Roses Every Night* (Quality Press, London, 1948)

Morley, S. *Tales from the Hollywood Raj: The British, the Movies and Tinseltown* (Viking Press, New York, 1984)

Neagle, A. *There's Always Tomorrow* (W. H. Allen, London, 1974)

Ney, J. *The European Surrender: A Descriptive Study of the American Social and Economic Conquest* (Little, Brown and Co., Boston,1970)

Nichols, B. *Movies and Methods, Volume 2* (University of California Press, Los Angeles, 1985)

Ninkovich, F. A. *The Diplomacy of Ideas: United States Foreign Policy and Cultural Relations, 1938-1950* (Cambridge University Press, New York, 1981)

Orwell, G. *The English People* (Collins, London, 1947)

_____ *England, Your England* (Secker and Warburg, London, 1953)

Pelling, H. M. *The Labour Governments, 1945-1951* (Macmillan, London, 1984)

Perry, G. *Movies from the Mansion: A History of Pinewood Studios* (Hamish Hamilton, London, 1976)

_____ *The Great British Picture Show* (Pavilion Press, London, 1985)

Political and Economic Planning, *The British Film Industry* (PEP, London, 1952)

_____, *The British Film Industry* (PEP, London, 1958)

Powdermaker, H. *Hollywood, the Dream Factory: An Anthropologist Looks at the Movie Makers* (Little and Brown and Co., Boston, 1950)

Pronay N. and Spring, D.W. (eds.) *Propaganda, Politics and Film, 1918-1945* (MacMillan, London, 1982)

Reisman, D., Glazer N. and Denney, R. *The Lonely Crowd : A Study of the Changing American Character* (Yale University Press, New Haven, 1950)

Richards, J. *Britain in the Age of the Picture Palace; Britain and Cinema, 1930 - 1939* (Routledge and Kegan Paul, London, 1984)

_____ *Visions of Yesterday* (Routledge and Kegan Paul, London, 1973)

Roddick, N. *A New Deal in Entertainment: Warner Brothers in the 1930s* (British Film Institute, London, 1983)

Rose, R. (ed.), *Lessons From America: An Exploration* (John Wiley, New York, 1974).

Rosenberg, E. *Spreading the American Dream: American Economic and Cultural Expansionism, 1890-1945* (Hill and Wang, New York, 1981)

Sayre, N. *Running Time: Films of the Cold War* (Dial Press, New York, 1982)

Seldes, G. *The Movies Come from America* (Charles Scribner, New York, 1937)

_____ *The Great Audience* (Viking Press, New York, 1950)

Servan-Schreiber, J. J. *The American Challenge* (Atheneum, New York, 1968)

Skidelsky, R. and Bogdanor, V. *The Age of Affluence* (Penguin, London, 1970)

Slide, A. (ed) *International Film, Radio and Television Journals* (Greenwood Press, London, 1985)

Snowman, D. *Britain and America: An Interpretation of Their Culture, 1945-1975* (New York University Press, New York, 1977)

Social Survey, *Children and the Cinema* (Central Office of Information, London, 1948)

Spraos, J. *The Decline of the Cinema: An Economist's Report* (Allen and Unwin, London, 1962)

Thomas, T. *Hollywood and the American Image* (Arlington House, New York, 1981)

Tudor, A. *Image and Influence; Studies in the Sociology of Film* (St Martin's Press, New York, 1975)

UNESCO, *The Old and the New World : Their Cultural and Moral Relations* (UNESCO, New York, 1954)

Vanderschmidt, F. *What the English Think of Us* (McBride, New York, 1948)

Visson, A. *As Others See Us* (Doubleday, Garden City, N.J., 1948)

Waites, B., Bennett, T. and Martin, G. *Popular Culture: Past and Present* (Croom Helm, Beckenham, 1983)

Walker, A. *Stardom: The Hollywood Phenomenon* (Stein and Day, New York, 1970)

Watt, D. C. *Succeeding John Bull: America in Britain's Place, 1900-1975* (Cambridge University Press, London, 1984)

Williams, F. *The Triple Challenge: The Future of Socialist Britain* (Heinemann, London, 1948)

_____ *The American Invasion* (Crown, New York, 1962)

Wilson, H. *A Prime Minister on Prime Ministers* (Summit Books, New York, 1977)

Wolfenstein, M. and Leites, N. *Movies; A Pyschological Study* (Free Press, Glencoe, 1950)

Wood, A. *Mr Rank* (Hodder and Stoughton, London, 1952)

Periodical Articles

Abrams, M. 'The British Cinema Audience', *Hollywood Quarterly*, vol. 3, no. 2 (1947-8)

Baker, B. 'Picturegoes', *Sight and Sound*, vol. 53, no. 3 (1985)

Browning, H. E. and Sorrell, A. A. 'Cinemas and Cinema-going in Great Britain', *Journal of the Royal Statistical Society*, vol. 117, pt. 2 (1954)

Buscombe, E. 'Film History and the Idea of a National Cinema', *Australian Journal Of Screen Theory*, nos. 9/10 (1981)

Carroll, R. "Selecting Motion Pictures For The Foreign Market', *Journal of Marketing*, vol. 17, no. 2 (1952)

Carstairs, J. P. 'All This and Export Too', *Film Industry: Monthly Review of Film Production*, vol. 1, no. 1 (July, 1946), p. 1.

Dawson, A. 'British and American Motion Picture Wage Rates Compared', *Hollywood Quarterly*, vol. 3, no. 3 (1948)

Elkin, F. 'The Value Implications in Popular Films', *Sociology and Social Research*, no. 38 (1954), pp. 320-2

England, L. 'What the Cinema Means to the British Public', *The Year's Work in Film* (1949)

Golden N. D. and Young, E. H. 'World Survey Shows Record Foreign Business', *Foreign Commerce Weekly*, 28 February 1955

Greiner, G. 'Children and the Cinema', *Christus Rex*, July 1954

Griffith, R. 'Where are the Dollars?' 1, *Sight and Sound*, December 1949

_____ 'Where are the Dollars?' 2, *Sight and Sound*, January 1950

Harrisson, T. 'British Opinion Moves Toward a New Synthesis',
  Public Opinion Quarterly, vol. 11, no. 3 (1947), pp. 327-41

Henderson, B. 'A Musical Comedy of Empire', *Film Quarterly*,
  Winter, 1981-2.

Johnston, E. 'Messengers from a Free Country', *Saturday Review of
  Literature*, 4 March 1950

Katz, R. 'Projecting America Through Films', *Hollywood Quarterly*,
  vol. 4, no. 3 (1950)

Koppes C. R. and Black, G. D. 'What To Show The World: The
  Office of War Information and Hollywood, 1942-1945', *Journal of
  American History*, no. 64 (1977), pp. 87 - 105.

Kracauer, S. 'National Types as Hollywood Presents Them',
  Public Opinion Quarterly, vol. 13, no. 3, (1949), pp. 53 -72

Lambert, R. 'Films and the Idea of Happiness', *Good Living* (1948)

MacCann, R. D. 'Subsidy for the Screen: Grierson and Group Three,
  1951-1955', *Sight and Sound*, vol. 46, no. 3 (1977)

Manvell, R. 'Clearing the Air', *Hollywood Quarterly*,
  vol. 1, no. 2 (1947)

_____ 'The Cinema and the State: England', *Hollywood Quarterly*,
vol. 2, no. 3 (1947), pp. 289-93

Rogow, A. A. 'The Public Relations Program of the Labour
Government and British Industry', *Public Opinion Quarterly*,
  vol. 16, no. 2 (1952)

Spitzer, H. M. 'Presenting America in American Propaganda',
  Public Opinion Quarterly, vol. 11, no. 2 (1947), pp. 213-21

Strauss, D. 'The Rise of Anti-Americanism in France: French
Intellectuals and the American Film Industry, 1927-1932',
  Journal of Popular Culture, vol. 19 (1977), pp. 753-9

Wall W. D. and Simson, W. A. 'The Effects of Cinema Attendance on
  the Behaviour of Adolescents As Seen by Their Contemporaries',
  British Journal of Educational Pyschology, vol. 19, 1949, pp. 53-61

Wanger, W. '120,000 Ambassadors', *Foreign Affairs*, vol. 18, no. 1,
  (1939)

_____ 'Donald Duck and Diplomacy', *Public Opinion Quarterly*,
  vol. 14, no. 2 (1950)

Periodicals

Board of Trade Journal
British Picture News
The Economist
Film Industry
Film Mirror
Foreign Affairs
Hollywood Quarterly
Photoplay
Pinewood Merry-Go-Round
Sight and Sound

Newspapers

New York Times
The Times
Wall Street Journal

INDEX

Abrams, Mark 4, 25, 46-7
Adams, Richard 54
Addison, Paul 37, 45, 109
advertising 4, 19-20, 46-7
Alexander, Norah 73
Alpert, Hollis 78
Americanization 2-5, 13-28, 140-1,
    151-2
    effects of 51-64
Anglo-American Film Agreement
    101-2
anti-Americanism 3, 14-17, 107-8,
    145
Arnold, Matthew 13, 16
art, film as 21-2, 51
Associated British Picture
    Corporation (ABPC) 83, 132,
    138, 149
Attenborough, Richard 73, 77
Attlee, Clement 26, 34, 88-9
Auden, W. H. 20
audiences, film 7, 150
    and stars 7, 67-79
    preferences of 31, 38-41, 150
    see also opinion polls
austerity, post-war 6-7, 22, 32-5,
    40

Barr, Charles 57
Barthes, Roland 67, 71
Beatles, the 27
Benjamin, Walter 19
Bernstein, Sidney 38-9, 82
    questionnaires 38, 75
Beveridge, William, Lord 88
Biskind, Peter 56, 58
Bogarde, Dirk 76-7

Boothby, Robert, Lord 86-7
boycott on Britain 10, 90-102
Bracken, Brendon 134
Brantlinger, Patrick 14, 16
British Film Producers Association
    133
British Film Production Fund 135
British Lion Film Corporation
    134, 136
Brogan, D. W. 14, 19
Buffalo Bill 18
Buffon, George-Louis de 16
bureaucracy 33-4
Burt, Sir Cyril 52
Buscombe, Ed 6

Carstairs, John Paddy 42
Chappell, Connery 71
Churchill, Sir Winston 109
Cinematograph Films Acts 9,
    38-9, 84, 98
class 27-8, 44
    see also working class
clothes 42-3
Cold War 2, 18, 108, 110
communism 113, 120
consensus 56-8
consumerism 26, 28, 43-5, 69-70
    151-2
co-operation, Anglo-American 8-9
cosmetics, use of 43, 47
Cowdin, Cheever 90
Cowles, Virginia 112
Cripps, Sir Stafford 23, 132
culture
    'high' 15, 20-1
    mass 13-15, 18
    US vs. European 14-18, 20

US government policy 105-23
youth 25
Cunliffe-Lister, Sir Philip 20

Dalton, Hugh 22-3, 85
D'Arne, Wilson 76
Davenport, Nicholas 136
delinquency 25, 52, 54
democracy 13-14, 16
Dickinson, Margaret 127
documentaries 21, 147
Durgnat, Raymond 56-7, 63, 77
Dyer, Richard 68-9, 71, 74
Eady, Sir Wilfred 137-8
Eady Levy 135
Ealing films 57, 63, 149
economy, British 24, 26, 85-9
  106-7, 114
Eliot, T.S. 15, 16, 28
embargo on films 90-102
emigration 23, 27
Empire Marketing Board 136-7
escapism 21, 40
Europe, culture 14-18, 20
European Recovery Program 91

family life 57-8
fans 7-8, 46, 70-5
Feuer, Jane 59
Fields, Gracie 44, 76
Film Finance Company 133-4
Film Production Council 84, 132
film-going 4, 6, 36-7, 138-9
  see also audiences; opinion polls
financing, film 23, 37, 127-8,
  132-6
Formby, George 44, 76
Friedman, Norman L. 52
Friese-Greene, William 130
Fuller, Walter R. 37, 92

Gaitskell, Hugh 23, 37, 133
Gallup, George 10, 27
  Polls 86, 93
Gans, Herbert 10, 28, 63-4, 78
Garbo, Greta 71
genre films 52, 56, 59-61
Goldcrest 153
Golden, Nathan 88, 116
Granger, Stewart 75-6, 82
Great Britain
  as market for US films 6, 9, 19,
    22, 31, 36, 84, 115
  economy of 24, 26, 85-9,
    106-7, 114
  film images of 35, 61-3, 129
  film production in 21, 38-9,
    63-4, 82-5, 92-4, 131, 140,
    147-9
  government of
    and film production 83-4
    and financing 23, 37, 127,
      132-6
    and US films 9-10, 82, 87,
      89-102
    film policy 10, 98-100, 127-
      41
Grierson, John 115, 122, 137-8,
  149
Griffith, Richard 96
Guback, Thomas 26, 131

Handel, Leo 70
Haralovitch, Mary Beth 75
Hays, Will B. 19-20, 116
Hecht, Ben 58, 120-1
Henderson, Brian 56
Hoggart, Richard 5, 25, 140-1
Hollywood 1, 19
Holtby, Winifred 44
Hooson, Tom 152
Hopkins, Harry 23, 44

Hulton Research Organization 36, 40, 42-5

Iddon, Don 107
ideology, US film 51-64
images, film
  of Great Britain 5, 61-3, 129
  of USA 5, 43-6, 53-7
industrialization 13-14, 16
Informational Media Guaranty
  Program 105, 122-3
International Motion Pictures
  Division, US State Department
  122

James, Henry 20
Johnston, Eric 55, 86-7, 90-1,
  100, 114-15
Jowett, Garth 70-1
Jungk, Robert 151

Katz, Robert 122
Keynes, John Maynard 111
Klein, Josephine 140, 150
Knight, Arthur 97
Korda, Sir Alexander 94, 133-4
Korda, Michael 130
Korea 24, 60, 106, 108
Kracauer, Siegfried 35, 62, 118

Laemmle, Carl 68
Lambert, Gavin 43, 61
Lancaster, Burt 58, 78
language 44
Lawrence, D. H. 16
Lawrie, J. H. 134, 137
Lazarus, Paul 96
Leavis, F. R. 15-16, 20-1

Leavis, Q. D. 15
Lejeune, C.A. 93
Levi-Strauss, Claude 52
Lewis, Sinclair 17
literature 15-16, 21-2
loans, from USA to Britain 23,
  27, 33-4, 86-8, 111-12
Low, Rachel 36
Lowenthal, Leo 69

magazines, cinema 41-2, 68
  fan 7-8, 70, 72, 75
Maltby, Richard 56
Manvell, Roger 83
markets for films:
  for US films 81-2, 115-18, 145
  Britain as 6, 9, 19, 22, 31, 36
    84, 115; embargo 81-102
  USA as market for British films
    94-8
Mason, James 75-6, 79, 82
mass culture 13-15, 18
Mass Observation surveys 40, 111
Mayer, J.P. 39-41, 43, 45, 57,
  74-5
'meaning' of films 5-6
men 42-3, 70-1
  stars 77-8
Meyer, Karl 27
Mills, John 77, 79
Morgan, Guy 4
Morley, Sheridan 8
Motion Picture Association of
  America (MPPA) 52, 86-90,
  93, 98-101, 116
Motion Picture Export Association
  (MPEA) 55, 87, 105, 114-15,
  117
Moyne Committee 116
Mulvey, Laura 71
musicals 59

myth 52-3

National Film Finance Corporation 133-7
Neagle, Anna 76
'negative classicism' 16
Ney, John 24
Olivier, Sir Laurence 96-7
opinion polls 10, 38-43, 82, 86, 93, 111
Orwell, George 18, 22, 110-11

Palache Committee 132
Palestine 35, 106, 120-1
Paramount Decrees 81, 95, 117
philosophy, national 2-3
Pickles, Wilfred 44
Piovene, Guido 2
policy
  British, film 10, 23, 37, 127-41
  British, protectionist 9-10, 82-4 87, 89-102
  US cultural 105-23
polls *see* opinion polls; *also* surveys
Potter, Jim 13
Priestley, J.B. 18
'progressivism' 141
propaganda 2, 10, 120
  see also US government cultural policy
protectionism 9-10, 86-91
psychoanalytic theory 8

quota system 9, 84-5, 129-31
Rank, J. Arthur 89, 127, 130-4
Rank Organization 39, 75-9, 82-3, 94, 97, 100, 132-5, 138, 147
rationing 24, 32

Rawnsley, David 92
Reith, Lord 134
Roddick, Nick 56
Roosevelt, Franklin D. 109
Rose, Billy 33
Rotherwyck, Lord 112
Russia 18, 107, 111, 117
  see also Cold War

Servan-Schreiber, Jacques 24
Social Survey 36, 40
socialism 26, 33-4, 109-10
Spengler, Oswald 16, 17
Spraos, John 138, 150
'standardization' 2, 17, 22
stars 67-79
  and audiences 7, 46
  British 7, 75-9, 82
  characters 70-5
  stardom 67-9
Steel, Anthony 77
Street, Sarah 127
structuralism 52
surveys, social 25, 45, 141
  film-going 36
  see also opinion polls
taxation
  entertainment 32, 89, 136
  luxuries 32
  US films 9, 89-91, 100
technology
  communications 3, 146, 153
  industrial 13-14
television 138, 141, 145-6, 150
Thompson, 21
Todd, Richard 77
Toqueville, Alexis, Comte de 39
Toynbee, Arnold 16
Truman, Harry S. 91, 108-10
Tudor, Andrew 72

UNESCO 15, 17, 118
Union of Soviet Socialist
 Republics
 (USSR) 18, 107, 111, 117
 see also Cold War
United States of America (USA)
 and British films 94-8
 film images of 5, 43-6, 53-7
 government:
  and US film industry 91,
  114-23
  cultural policy 105-23
  propaganda 10, 120
 values 52-4
Vanderschmidt, Fred 107-8, 113,
 121
video recorders 153
Vinson, Fred 111
Visson, Andre 2, 15, 53, 113

Wanger, Walter 2, 55, 71, 118-19
Waugh, Evelyn 61
Webb-Pomerene Act 116-17
Wenders, Wim 150
westerns 59
Wheare Committee 37
White, Walter 122
Wilcox, Herbert 76
Wilding, Michael 76
Williams, Francis 3, 5
Williams, Raymond 5
Williams, Robin 52
Wilmott, Paul 25
Wilson, Sir Harold 23, 37, 98-9,
 101, 133
women 42-3, 70-1
Wood, Alan 136
working class 4
 and Americanization 18, 25,
 27-8

film preferences 37, 46
 speech 44
 view of USA 18, 45-6
Wright Will 52, 59

Yalta conference 110
Young, Michael 25
young people 25, 42, 44